POCKET
BIBLE
DICTIONARY

NELSON'S
POCKET
REFERENCE™
SERIES

POCKET
BIBLE
DICTIONARY

Defining the Bible A-Z

Over 1,500 Entries

THOMAS NELSON
Since 1798

THOMAS NELSON

Copyright © 1978, 1999 by Thomas Nelson, Inc

Copyright © by Nelson-National

Published by Thomas Nelson, 501 Nelson Place, Nashville, TN 37214, USA. Thomas Nelson is a registered trademark of HarperCollins Christian Publishing, Inc.

Requests for information should be addressed to customercare@harpercollins.com.

Thomas Nelson titles may be purchased in bulk for educational, business, fund-raising, or sales promotional use. For information, please email SpecialMarkets@ ThomasNelson.com.

ISBN 978-0-310-18111-8 (Softcover)

The Library of Congress has Catalogued the previous edition as:

Nelson's pocket reference Bible dictionary.
     p.   cm.
    ISBN 1-4185-0016-X
    1. Bible—Dictionaries. I. Thomas Nelson Publishers. II. Title: Pocket reference Bible dictionary.
  BS440.N349 1999   99–18407
  220.3—dc21   CIP

HarperCollins Publishers, Macken House, 39/40 Mayor Street Upper, Dublin 1, D01 C9W8, Ireland (https://www.harpercollins.com)

Printed in the United States of America

25 26 27 28 29 30 31 32 33 /VPI/ 12 11 10 9 8 7 6 5 4 3 2

FOREWORD

A Bible dictionary is an indispensable reference tool for everyone interested in learning more about the Bible. The Bible is an important foundation of western civilization and references to it appear frequently in literature, history, and newspapers and magazine articles.

The conciseness and handy size of this Bible dictionary make it uniquely useful to both the average reader and the Bible student. You can use it at home or carry it to Sunday school or Bible study where it can become a reference tool for the whole class. The illustrations make many of the words come alive by picturing what cannot be described easily.

Whenever you want to know more about the Bible, turn to this handy dictionary. Wherever you carry your Bible, you should also take along NELSON'S POCKET REFERENCE BIBLE DICTIONARY.

A

Aa'ron

The elder brother of and often the spokesman for Moses. From him descended, through his son Eleazer, the hereditary class of priests in Israel.

Ab

The 5th month of the Hebrew year. *See* Calendar.

Ab'ba

A name addressed to God in Jewish and early Christian prayers. It occurs three times in the NT, with its Greek equivalent placed after it (Mk 14.36; Rom 8.15; Gal 4.6).

A·bed'ne·go

The Babylonian name of one of the companions of Daniel, his Hebrew name being Azariah. *See* Shadrach.

A'bel

(Heb. "vanity," "breath"; Akkad. "son") 1. The second son of Adam, who was murdered by his brother Cain (Gen 4.2ff). He was God-fearing and righteous, and in contrast with Cain is a pattern of a worshiper pleasing to God, who on that account has to suffer (1 Jn 3.12). He is described as righteous by our Lord (Mt 23.35), and in Heb 11.4 he stands at the head of the heroes of faith.

2. Part of the name of several places in Israel; it probably signifies "plain" or "meadow." *Abel of Beth-maacah,* a fortified city, identified with the mound Tell Abil, 12 mi. N of Lake Huleh,

extreme north of Israel (2 Sam 20.14-19). *Abel-keramim*, the plain of the vineyards, in Ammonite territory, probably near modern Amman (Judg 11.29-33). *Abel-meholah*, probably east of the Jordan on Wadi el-Yabis, modern Tell el-Maqlub (Judg 7.22; 1 Kings 4.12; 19.16). *Abel-mizraim*, possibly between Jericho and the Dead Sea (Gen 50.11). *Abel-shittim*, in the plains of Moab NE of the Dead Sea; possibly the present Tell el Hammam. Early name for Shittim (Num 33.49).

A·bi'a·thar

(Heb. "the Father [God] gives abundantly") A priest who became the priest of David.

A'bib

(Heb. "young head of grain") The 1st month of the Hebrew year; Nisan. *See* Calendar.

Ab'i·gail

(Heb. "my father rejoices") Wife of Nabal and after Nabal's death the wife of David.

A·bim'e·lech

(Heb. "Melek is Father") 1. A king of Gerar who appears in similar accounts of Isaac and Rebecca and of Abraham and Sarah (Gen 20–21; 26).

2. Son of Jerubbaal (Gideon), king of Shechem (Judg 8.31; 9.1-57).

Ab'ner

(Heb. "father is Ner") Commander of the Israelite army under Saul.

a·bom·i·na'tion

Anything ritually or ethically repugnant or loathsome to God and men.

A·bra·ham, A·bram

(Heb. "Father of a multitude"; "exalted Father") One of the greatest OT characters (Gen 11.27–25.8). Abraham was born in Ur of the Chaldees, in what is now Iraq. Terah, his father, migrated with Abraham and Sarah, Abraham's wife, and Lot, his nephew, as far as Harah, now Harran, in Turkey. There Terah died. The others, with flocks and herds, moved on to Palestine (Canaan).

Abraham stopped near ancient Shechem, a short distance E of Nablus and now extensively excavated; he moved on to Egypt for a time, then returned to Palestine for the remainder of his life. Lot settled at Sodom and became a Canaanite. When the Canaanites rebelled against Babylon and Lot was taken captive, Abraham recovered the captives and the booty.

Throughout his life, Abraham was in contact with the many peoples about him, carrying on various negotiations with them. He talked with God, to whom he was always faithful. And he doubted God when he and his wife Sarah were in their old age promised a son. This son was Isaac. However, Abraham's relationship with God was such that when he was called upon to sacrifice his only son he responded without question. God released him from the sacrifice and promised him many descendants and land, which promises were fulfilled.

At Sarah's death he arranged the purchase of a burial place at Machpelah, where he also was buried after a long life of constant activity and great drama.

Ab′sa·lom

(Heb. "father of peace") Son of David and Maachah, through popular arts alienating the people from his father, at length raised a revolt against him, but was defeated by Joab and slain by him, to the great sorrow of David (2 Sam 3.3, 13.20–19.10).

a·ca′cia

A tree providing a hard wood, useful in building.

Ac′cad

(Gen 10.10) One of the four cities of Nimrod in Shinar (Babylonia). Land of Sumer and Accad (or Akkad) is in the Assyrian inscriptions the common designation of Babylonia as a whole. *See* Akkad; Babylonia.

A·cel′da·ma, A·kel′da·ma

A burial ground outside the Jerusalem wall.

Acts of the A·pos′tles, The

Written by the author of the Gospel according to Luke, Acts is the account of what Jesus' disciples did after His resurrection. It tells about the early Christian church and its missionaries, the baptism of Cornelius, the Council in Jerusalem, and about the conversion of Paul and his journeys to establish churches and to teach. Acts emphasizes that the church is guided continually by the Holy Spirit.

Ad′am

("earthy," "a human") 1. The Hebrew word for man, specifically applied to the first man.

Created on the same day as the animals, he is not semi-divine but has the ability for spiritual growth.

2. A city east of the Jordan, now Tell ed-Damiyeh (Josh 3.9-17).

ad'a·mant

It is not known what is meant by this word; it is something impenetrably hard (Ezek 3.9; Jer 17.1; Zech 7.12).

A'dar, Ad'dar

The 12th Hebrew month. *See* Calendar.

Ad·on·i'

A Hebrew name for God.

Ad·o·ra'im

(Heb. "two threshing floors"?) A city identified with modern Dura, 5 mi. W-SW of Hebron (2 Chron 11.9).

A·dul'lam

(Heb. "retreat, refuge") Extensive ruins in the Wadi es-Sur, 9½ mi. ENE of Beit Jibrin, perhaps mark the site of Adullam, to which there are many biblical references.

a·ga'pe, the

(Gr. agape, "love") Love feasts, the common meals of the early Christians, which expressed the brotherly love that bound them together as one family, and culminated in the Lord's Supper. Gross abuses of this beautiful custom, such as are condemned in 1 Cor 11.17ff, and Jude 12, led to the separation of the Lord's Supper from the love feast in the post-apostolic church.

ag'ate

The agate is one of the many varieties of minutely crystalline silica, denoting those arranged more or less in bands of different tints. From a very early period it has been used as a gem, and was often engraved.

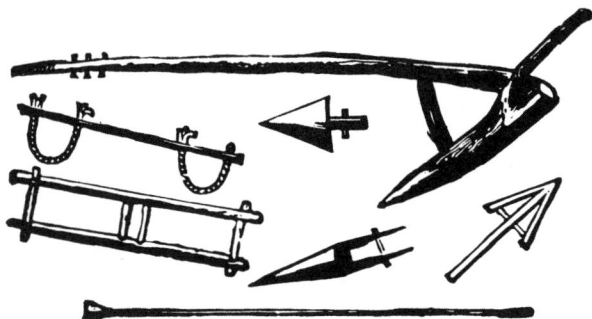

Plow and other implements

ag'ri·cul·ture

Excavations reveal a developed agriculture in Bible lands as early as 8000-7000 B.C.; flint sickles for harvesting and basalt mortars and pestles for grinding grain are found in abundance. The religious year of the Israelites was adjusted to the cultivation cycle, and many memorable passages of the Bible have reference to the life of seedtime and harvest.

The patriarchs and their descendants down to the conquest of Canaan were herdsmen of cattle (sheep, oxen, goats, asses, and camels). After the settlement, the western tribes learned agriculture, and the culture of the vine, olive, and fig tree, from the Canaanites. Among the crops raised were wheat, barley, rye, spelt, flax, cummin, fitches or vetch, beans, lentils, and millet.

A'hab

(Heb. "father's brother") Son of Omri, king of the northern kingdom of Israel in the time of Elijah, reigned 22 years. He defeated Ben-Hadad, King of Damascus, twice, destroyed his capital, and shut him up in Aphek, afterward forming a treaty with him against Assyria. Shalmaneser II, King of Assyria, in his monolith inscription claims to have defeated Ahab and Ben-Hadad with other kings at Karkar in 854 B.C. A year after this, Ahab met his death in a battle before Ramoth Gilead, in which Ben-Hadad overcame both him and his ally, Jehoshaphat of Judah. The worship of Baal and Ashtoreth, introduced by his wife, the Tyrian princess, Jezebel, with the religious struggle this called forth in the country, and his robbery and judicial murder of Naboth, left in Israel a dark shadow on the memory of Ahab (1 Kings 16.29–22.40).

A·has·u·e'rus

The Persian king (485-465 B.C.?) in Ezra 4.6 and Esther. The Ahasuerus of Dan 9.1 is the father of Darius the Mede.

A'haz

(Heb. "possessor" or "be has grasped") Eleventh king of Judah, remembered for his wicked reign (2 Kings 16, 23.12; 2 Chron 28; Is 7,8,9).

A·ha·zi'ah
(Heb. "Yah has grasped") 1. Eighth king of Israel.

2. Sixth king of Judah.

A·hi'jah, A·hi'ah
(Heb. "brother of Yah") Name of 9 persons in the OT, one of whom was a priest in the time of Saul; another a prophet of Shiloh who foretold Jeroboam's kingship.

A·him'a·az
(Heb. "brother is counselor"?) Name of 3 persons in the OT, one of whom was a priest devoted to David.

A·hin'o·am
(Heb. "pleasantness") 1. Wife of Saul, daughter of Ahimaaz.

2. A wife of David, from Jezreel.

A·hith'o·phel
The royal counselor to David.

Ai'ja·lon, Aj'a·lon
(Heb. "place of the deer") 1. Modern Yalo, with remains of a fortified town.

2. A place in Zebulun, probably Tell el-Butneh in the Plain of Asochis.

Ak'kad, Ak·ka'di·an
The Akkadians were the first Semitic people to move into Mesopotamia; the first Akkadian names to appear among Babylonian rulers are found in the period 1200-1100 B.C. Their language had spread widely and had become the common usage for commerce and trade some 750 years earlier. Assyrian and Babylonian are considered dialects of Akkadian.

Alabaster vessels

al'a·bas·ter

A soft stone, often veined; light cream in color.
Much used for perfume flasks.

Al·ex·an'dri·a

The great seaport at the mouth of the Nile,
founded by Alexander the Great about 332 B.C.
He gave the Jews a quarter in it; in the early
Christian age it was the chief trade center of
East and West, and the home of literature and
Greek philosophy.

al'gum

(2 Chron 2.8, 9.10, 11) or **al'mug** (1 Kings 2.8,
10.11, 12) A wood brought from Lebanon, as in
2 Chron 2.8, or from Ophir (1 Kings; 2 Chron
9.10, 11). Probably either pine or sandalwood.

Almond tree and blossoms

al'mond
(Heb. "waking") The common almond, whose beautiful pink-white flowers appear in January, the first of the year; hence its name. It grows wild on the higher lands of Palestine. There are frequent references to this tree in the Bible.

alms
(Gr. "pity"; "relief of the poor") Frequently mentioned and their giving practiced in many ways. Laws were written, tithes were taken with the poor in mind. Gleaning was usual. Passersby might gather as they walked. And the giving of alms meant merit for the donor.

al'mug
See Algum.

Courtesy of *The Interpreter's
Dictionary of the Bible*

Aloes

al'oes

1. An aromatic substance, probably an aromatic wood, such as white sandalwood, from which was made incense and perfume. It was an import, not native.

2. The true aloe, a succulent, provided a bitter and evil-smelling purgative and may have been used with myrrh in embalming.

al'pha and o·me'ga

The names of the first and last letters in the Greek alphabet. "Alpha and Omega" often indicates the whole extent, not merely the beginning and the end, of an act or a concept.

Al·phae'us

A Greek name appearing in the NT only. 1. The father of Levi, who may also have been called Matthew (Mk 2.14).

2. The father of James (the Less) (Mt 10.3; Mk 3.18; Lk 6.15; Acts 1.13).

al'tar

An artificial erection for the offering of sacrifices and prayers, originally of earth, turf, and unhewn stones. The law ordained that sacrifices should be offered only in the sanctuary; but the Hebrews continued to erect altars upon the high places until the Temple at Jerusalem, with its altar of incense in the sanctuary and its altar of burnt-offering in the forecourt, became under the reformation of Josiah universally recognized as the only place where sacrifices could be legitimately offered. The "horns" of the altar, placed at its four corners, were its most sacred parts. The blood of the sacrifices was smeared on them, and they were clasped by fugitives who claimed the right of asylum.

Am'a·lek·ites

A nomadic tribe, descendants of Esau, wandering from Sinai across the Negev, below the Sea of Galilee, as far as the Gulf of Aqabah. They warred with the Israelites over the centuries. Saul and David defeated them, but neither suc-

ceeded in exterminating them. At the time of
Hezekiah they seem to have been completely
defeated. In the Tell el-Amarna letters, they are
classed as plunderers.

Am·a·sa
(Heb. "a burden") 1. A nephew of David.
2. An Ephraimite chief.

Am·a·zi'ah
(Heb. "Yah is strong") The name of 4 persons
in the OT, one a king of Judah, presumably for
29 years.

am'ber
The word thus rendered is almost certainly not
the familiar fossil resin of orange-yellow, which
bears this name, but some metallic compound;
possibly the mixture of gold and silver now
called electrum, or bronze.

a'men'
A Hebrew word meaning "truth," used adverbi-
ally to express strong confirmation. It is used
as a confirmatory response at the close of prayer
("May it be so").

am'e·thyst
A purplish variety of quartz (crystallized silica),
often used for ornamental purposes. It looks
like a pale purple glass, but is somewhat harder.

Am'mon·ites
A Semitic people settled NE of the Dead Sea.
They warred with Israel, were vassals under
David and Solomon, subsequently vassals of
Assyria. Origen mentioned them in the 3rd cen-
tury A.D., after which they seem to have dis-

appeared among the Arabs. Excavations near Amman show a well-developed culture.

A'mon

(Heb. "reliable") Name of 3 persons in the OT, one a king of Judah; also the imperial god of Egypt.

Am'o·rites

An ancient people who may have occupied Syria and N Palestine; their language was probably the forerunner of Aramean. They refused the Israelites passage through their land. The Tell elAmarna letters give information of them at the period of a number of city states; excavations at Mori show a high state of civilization.

A'mos

(Heb. "burden bearer") One of the minor prophets, he was a shepherd of Tekoa, in Judah, and prophesied at Bethel in the reigns of Uzziah, King of Judah, and Jeroboam II, King of Israel. The priests accused him of treason, and expelled him from the northern kingdom, to which his prophecies mainly refer, and whose downfall he foretold.

A'mos, The Book of

The book of the herdsman from Tekoa. He received a direct call from God to prophesy against the unrighteousness of both Judah and Israel. Amos was the first prophet to proclaim that God was the ruler of the whole universe.

An'a·kim

(Heb. "people of the neck") A race of giants who, when driven from the mountains of Hebron by Caleb or Joshua, found refuge in Philistia.

An·a·ni'as

(Heb. "Yah is gracious") Name of 3 NT persons, one of whom was the high priest before whom Paul was tried in Jerusalem. Another lost his life for attempting deceit regarding the price received for property he sold.

a·nath'e·ma

(Gr. "something set up") One form of the word developed a special meaning, "devoted to a divinity or to the lower world so as to be destroyed," and so came to mean accursed.

An'a·thoth

The birthplace of Jeremiah. The name is preserved in Anata, a town 3 mi. N of Jerusalem. The ancient city was at Ras el-Karrubeh, ½ mi. SW.

An'cient of Days

God Himself, of great dignity and wisdom.

an'cients

See Elders.

An'drew

(Gr. "manly") One of the 12 disciples of Jesus, brother of Simon Peter, son of Jonas or John, was born at Bethsaida on the Sea of Galilee. He was one of the first among the disciples of John the Baptist to become a follower of Jesus who called him, along with Peter, while fishing at the Sea of Galilee, to become a fisher of men. He appears to have been one of those disciples who, after Peter, James, and John, stood nearest to his Master. Acts mentions him only in

1.13. According to tradition, he suffered martyrdom in Achaia on a cross shaped in the form of the letter X (Mt 4:18, 10.2-4, 16.17; Mk 1.16-20, 29; 3.16-19, 13.3; Jn 1.35-42, 44; 6.5-9; 12.20-22; 21.15-17; Lk 5.10, 6.14-16; Acts 1.13).

an'gel
(Gr. "messenger") A messenger of God, with the evolving concept of a spiritual being.

an'ise
Seeds of this plant are used for flavoring, and have some use in medicine.

An'nas
See Caiaphas.

ant
Ants are proverbial for the marvelous instinct that guides them in the economy, work, and discipline of their communities. They are small insects, but have wonderful muscular strength. Harvester ants of Palestine store corn for winter (Prov 16.6-8; 30.25).

an'te·lope
The Hebrew word of the OT is also translated "wild bull," "wild ox." The gazelle, a species of antelope, lived in Palestine in biblical times. The antelope is often depicted on Egyptian monuments. It is a beautiful creature, standing about four feet high, very wild and fleet, and fierce when hard pressed by the hunter.

an'ti·christ
This word is used in the NT by John (1 Jn 2.18, 22; 4.3; 2 Jn 7) but the idea, variously expressed, appears as in Dan 7, Ezek 38 and 39, 2

Thess 2.3–10. As used in the NT the name may mean "one who usurps the place of Christ," or "one who sets himself up as a substitute for Christ." The principle of his opposition consists in the denial of the incarnation, which revealed the will of God to unite man with Himself through Christ, and in the assertion of man's divinity apart from God in Christ. St. Paul teaches that Antichrist will appear as a single adversary of Christ, "the man of sin," who, furnished by Satan "with all power, and signs, and wonders of falsehood," will sit "in the sanctuary of God, setting himself forth as God," and will be brought to nought by the manifestation of the coming of the Lord. As Moses was the type of Christ, so Balaam, the "Anti-Moses," was a type of Antichrist (2 Pet 2.15; Jude 11; Rev 2.14).

an'ti·mo·ny
Stibnite (antimony sulphide) was and still is in the East a pigment employed for darkening the outer part of the eye, as when Jezebel "painted" her eyes.

An'ti·och
1. In Syria, on the river Orontes, a great city, ranking next after Rome and Alexandria, where the name Christian was first used (Acts 11.26).

2. In Pisidia, visited by St. Paul and Barnabas (Acts 13.14-52).

An·tip'a·tris
A city 10 mi. NE of Jaffa (Joppa) named after Antipater, father of Herod the Great (Acts 23.31).

apes

Imported by Solomon (1 Kings 10.22). Baboons, apes, and monkeys are represented in the Assyrian and Egyptian monuments.

A'phek

(Heb. "fortress"?) The name of 4 places in the OT. Each location has been identified.

Ap·ol·lo'ni·a

A Greek city in Macedonia, S of Lake Balbe (Acts 17.1).

A·pol'los

An Alexandrian Jew who became a prominent teacher in the Apostolic ages. "Eloquent," "fervent in spirit," and "mighty in the Scriptures" (of the OT), he had been a disciple of John before Priscilla and Aquila at Ephesus "expounded to him the way of God more perfectly." After Paul's departure from Corinth he preached the gospel there. Though one of the parties in the Corinthian church named itself after him, he appears to have stood in a friendly relation to Paul, with whom he afterwards labored at Ephesus. He is last mentioned in Tit 3.13. Luther was the first to suggest that Apollos was the author of the Epistle to the Hebrews (Acts 18.24-28, 19.1; 1 Cor. 1.12, 3.3-10, 22; 4.6, 16.12).

a·pos'tle

(Gr. "to send off") The word appears about 80 times in the NT, limited to certain men of the first generation of the church and missionaries of the gospel. The first twelve apostles sent out by Jesus are named in Mk 3.14-19 and elsewhere. Others also are considered apostles, including Paul, James, Barnabas, Matthias, and in some groupings Junias, Andronicus, and Silvanus. Subsequently many claimed the title, which the church desired to limit to those who had seen Jesus and had firsthand knowledge of the Resurrection, who had the attributes called the signs of an apostle, and were fully committed to the church.

ap'ple

Since the apple grows poorly if at all in Bible lands, an attempt has been made to identify the fruit so called. The apricot seems best to fit the biblical text.

Aq'ui·la and Pris·cil'la

Friends in Corinth and Ephesus of the Apostle Paul, and his assistants in evangelism. In Ephesus they instructed the Alexandrian Apollos.

A·ra'bi·a, A·ra'bi·ans

(Gr. "desert") In biblical times there was no single name for the vast Arabian peninsula. Its peoples were nomads. They traded with Egypt and other countries, selling frankincense and other perfumes, and had camels, sheep, goats, and horses. They may have been dealers in the pet monkeys Solomon had brought from Ophir, of still unknown location. The peoples included Ishmaelites, Midianites, Dedanites, Sabeans, among others. At times they raided and plundered in Israel, at times carried on peaceful commerce. There was a marked difference in the peoples of the N and the S. Whether the Queen of Sheba came from N or S is not definite; more probably she was from the N. There was a certain amount of intermingling, too: for example, David's head camel keeper was an Ishmaelite, and his sister married an Ishmaelite. Moses had friendly contacts with them. Bible references to the peoples of what is now Arabia are plentiful.

A'ram

(Akkad. *Aramu*) The OT name of Syria and Mesopotamia (sometimes used of Syria alone).

Ar·a·ma'ic

The Aramaic language is properly the speech of the people of Aram, an area NE of Syria. They may have learned alphabetic writing from the Canaanites. After the Assyrian conquest Aramaic spread widely as a language of commerce and is found in conjunction with cuneiform on weights and clay tablets from distant regions of the empire. A form of Aramaic influenced the Greek alphabet, and other forms influenced scripts of Asia. It is noteworthy that Dan 2.4-7, 28; Ezra 4.8-6,18 and 7.12-26 are found originally in Aramaic. The language was used in Egypt, and it was spoken familiarly instead of Hebrew in Palestine; Jesus and his followers spoke one of its many dialects.

Eventually Aramaic was displaced by Arabic in much of the old Assyrian empire, even though in some regions it persisted for centuries.

Ar·a·me'ans

A Semitic people, traditionally descendants of Shem, they apparently were in early times

Roman soldier

among the nomads along the W side of the Syrian Desert. For a considerable time they were an active and expanding people, and their culture, particularly their language, spread over the Middle East. The Assyrians conquered and scattered them, and they vanished as a political power.

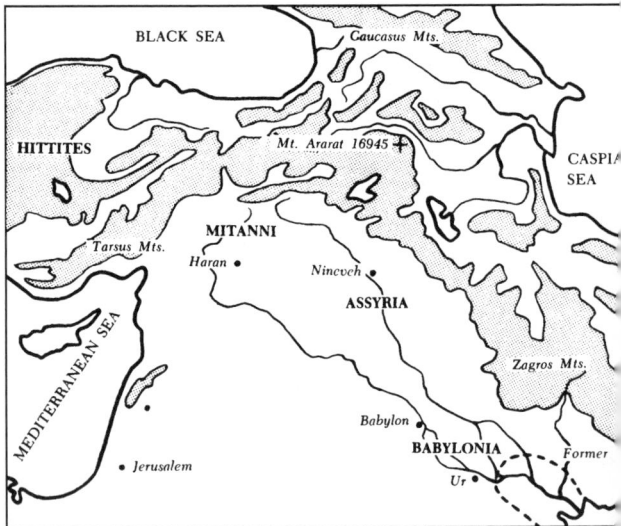

Location of Mt. Ararat.

Ar'a·rat
The country of the river Aras in Armenia; also the mount of Ararat, on which the ark rested after the Flood (Gen 8.4), 16,900 ft. elevation.

Ar·is·tar′chus

A Macedonian Gentile arrested with Paul in Ephesus. He traveled with Paul and was a fellow prisoner in Rome.

Ark of the Cov′e·nant

The ark may have been a container for the Mosaic tablets and other sacred objects, or a throne for the invisible God; on it was a slab of gold to support the cherubim, the mercy seat. It probably goes back to the time of Moses, and was a focus for the religious life of the people. In Ex 25 are precise instructions for the construction of an ark. The OT has some 200 references to it: it was captured in battle, left in the homes of individuals, reverenced, sometimes ignored. After Solomon placed it in the sanctuary of the temple it dropped from history. A possibility is that it was destroyed during Nebuchadnezzar's invasion.

Ar·ma·ged′don

The place of the final great struggle between the forces of good and evil. It is linked to Megiddo.

arm′lets

See Frontlets.

arms, ar′mor

Down to the age of David the army of Israel consisted exclusively of foot soldiers. These were probably divided into two classes: the heavy-armed, wearing helmet, coat of mail, and greaves, and carrying a sword, one or two javelins, and a spear; and the light-armed, wearing helmet and corselet of leather, and carrying

sword, bow, and sling. The metal earliest employed in the manufacture of weapons was
probably an alloy of copper and tin. The use of
imported iron followed later.

A sling

Ar′o·er

(Heb. "juniper"?) 1. A city on the N rim of the Arnon Gorge, 3 mi. SE of Dhiban. The ancient city is a mound beside modern 'Ara'ir.

   2. A town of Gilead, possibly S of 'Amman near es-Sweiwina.

   3. A town in S country of Judah, modern 'Ar'arah, 12 mi. SE of Beer-sheba.

Ar·tax·erx′es

The first Artaxerxes is mentioned in Ezra 7 and Neh 2 and 13. His grandson, Artaxerxes II, may have been the builder of the palace described in Esther 1.

Ar′te·mis

The virgin huntress of Greek classical mythology, called Diana by the Romans, was widely worshiped throughout the Greek world. Artemis or Diana of the Ephesians mentioned in Acts 19 was a fertility goddess, worship of whom was also widespread and elaborate.

As′ca·lon, Ash′ke·lon

One of the Philistine chief cities, on the seacoast. It may have been the birthplace of Herod the Great.

As·cents′, Songs of

See Degrees, Songs of.

Ash′dod

("fortress"?) A Philistine chief city, 10 mi. N of Ascalon (Ashkelon), and 3 mi. inland; now called Esdud. It was to Ashdod that the Ark was taken when captured by the Philistines.

A·she′rah

A Semitic fertility goddess and the goddess' cult

object, a sacred tree (for which a pole was often substituted) which, with the Masseba or sacred stone pillar, stood near the altar on every Canaanite high place. The deity was believed to be present in the Asherah. There are many OT references to the trees and the groves on the high places.

Ash′ke•lon
See Ascalon.

Ash′to•reth, pl. Ash′ta•roth, Ash′to•roth
A Canaanite fertility goddess.

As•mo•de′us
The prince of demons, also called Abaddon, Apollyon, Beelzebul.

asp
A viper or adder; a poisonous snake.

ass
The domesticated ass, which is traced by Darwin to the wild ass of Abyssinia, is depicted in the earliest Egyptian records, and also on the oldest Assyrian monuments. The ass is much more highly prized in the East than in the West. From early times, white (albino) asses were reserved for dignitaries. The ass was the animal of peace as the horse was of war. It was forbidden to plough with an ass and an ox together. *Ass, Wild* Most of the Biblical references are to the wild ass of Syria, especially the descriptions in Job and the Prophets. The wild ass is untamable, and in fleetness far surpasses the horse. The allusions to its habits in Scripture are most accurate. The hunting of the wild ass is

Ashtoreth

frequently represented in the Assyrian sculptures.

as·sas'sin

(Arab, *hashashin* "those addicted to hashish, hemp") A numerous body of desperadoes that arose in Judea during the procuratorship of Felix, and afterward took a leading part in the Jewish war. Their name Sicarii was derived from the curved dagger (Lat. *sica*), which they carried under their clothes, and with which they stabbed their opponents secretly in the crowds at festivals.

As'shur, As'sur

See Assyria.

As·syr'i·a

After the decline of the great kingdom of Sumer, two Semitic-language peoples developed in its region. Babylonia gradually rose in the former Central Sumer area. To the N of it Assyria developed, early unstable and unaggressive, borrowing heavily from Babylonia, but with sharp distinctions in social and intellectual concepts. Several strong personalities built up successive Assyrian empires, which in turn broke up on the death of the particular person. This was the Assyrian history for hundreds of years. They gradually conquered the mountain peoples N and E of them, and turned to the W. From the time of Omri (876-869 B.C.) to Manasseh (687-642 B.C.) the people of Israel were under pressure from Assyria: paying tribute to, fighting against, being conquered by Assyria; Tiglath-pileser II (966-935 B.C.), a contemporary of Solomon, was known to Israel, as was Shalmaneser III (858-824 B.C.), the first Assyrian king to have contact with the kings of Israel. Tiglath-pileser III (745-727) B.C.) began large-scale deportations of the conquered. Esarheddon (680-669 B.C.) attacked Egypt. The over-extended Assyrian empire fell with the destruction of Asshur, its old capital, in 614 B.C. and of Nineveh in 612 B.C. by a coalition of Babylonia and the Medes. A vast quantity of historical, artistic, and literary material has been found in the excavations of the ancient Assyrian cities in what is now Iraq, Turkey, and Syria, and many previously unsuspected links between the ancient peoples have been revealed.

Ath′ens

The capital of Attica, the chief division of ancient Greece, and the seat of Greek literature, art, and civilization. Paul visited it in his second journey and delivered a famous address on the Areopagus, or Hill of Mars.

Ath′ter

See Molech.

A·tone′ment, Day of

This was the annual day of humiliation and expiation for the sins of the nation, when the high priest made atonement for the sanctuary, the priests, and the people. It was celebrated on the 10th day of Tishri, the 7th month, by abstinence from ordinary labor, by a holy convocation, and by fasting. It was the only fast enjoined by the Mosaic law, and hence was called "the fast." The high priest, laying aside his official ornaments, first offered a sin-offering for himself and for the priesthood, entering into the Holy of Holies with the blood. He afterwards took 2 he-goats for the nation. One was slain for Jehovah. On the head of the other the sins of the people were typically laid; it was made the sin-bearer of the nation; and, laden with guilt, was sent away into the wilderness. The idea of atonement was never at any time remote.

Sin offering

a·veng'er

Hebrew custom, like that of many other early peoples, authorized and even required the next of kin to avenge a murdered person by killing his murderer. The Mosaic legislation aimed at mitigating its effects by providing cities of refuge to which a homicide might escape, and where he might claim a fair trial. Blood vengeance is mentioned often in the OT.

Az·a·ri'ah

(Heb. "Yah has helped") Name of 24 persons in the OT, one of whom was the prophet who encouraged Asa, king of Judah, to reform of religion. In 2 Chron 22.6, KJV, it is used instead of Ahaziah.

A·za'zel

The evil spirit of the wilderness to whom on the Day of Atonement the goat laden with the sins of the people is said to be sent.

B

Ba'al

The fertility gods of Canaan. There were many local Baals.

Ba'al·ze'bub

A god of the city of Ekron of the Philistines of whom King Ahaziah of Israel asked an oracle.

Ba'bel (Heb.), **Bab'y·lon** (Gr.)

Capital of Babylonia, or Shinar, also called Chaldea. Its ruins are near the present city of Hilla SW of Baghdad, on a small tributary of the Euphrates. Its temple of Bel (Marduk), the city God, a ziggurat or stepped tower, is the biblical Tower of Babel. It was a splendid and magnificent city, and became to the people of Israel a symbol of all that was wicked. In NT times it became the symbolic name for Rome.

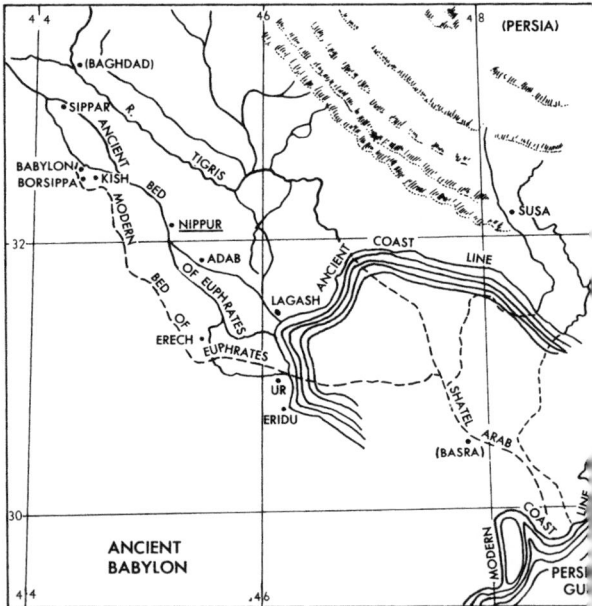

ANCIENT BABYLON

Bab·y·lo'ni·a

The downfall of Sumer brought Babylonia into being. The great Hammurabi (c. 1800-1750 B.C.) extended the power of his city-state, Babylon, making it a capital over other city-states. He was an effective administrator and estab-

lished an enduring political plan; even so, the
history of Babylonia is as that of Assyria, of
war and destruction, advance and retreat. The
complexities of the histories of both countries
are slowly being resolved through excavations
and subsequent interpretations of the records
found. The aggressions of Babylon are woven
through the history of the Israelites; there were
the sorrowful days of the exiles, when thousands of the people of Israel were deported
eastward, never to return. There were such hap-
penings as the three young men in the fiery
furnace (Dan 3). Lying as Israel did, between
Egypt and the Tigris-Euphrates powers, Assyria and Babylonia, it was a buffer or a pawn
in the multiple strife of the larger powers. But
Babylon emerged as the most hated. Babylon
was synonymous with all that was evil. It eventually became a part of the empire of the Medes
and Persians.

Bab·y·lo'ni·an Cap·tiv'i·ty or Ex'ile

The period in Jewish history from the carrying
away of the people to Babylon in 597 and 586
to their return in 538 B.C.

badg'er

A small mammal; a coney.

Ba'laam

("the clan brings forth"?) A seer, possibly from
the neighborhood of Carchemish, summoned by
the Moabite King Balak to pronounce a curse
on Israel before its entrance into Canaan. Instead he spoke a series of blessings (Num 22–
24). There are many references to Balaam in

both OT and NT; in the NT he becomes the false prophet.

Baker, from an ancient marble

balm
An aromatic gum or resin used in healing and in cosmetics as well as for embalming. It is not fully identified.

bal'sam
See Mulberry.

bap'tism
(Gr. "dip" or "immerse") A rite using water as a symbol of religious purification.

Ba'rak

(Heb. "lightning-flash") Son of Abinoam, who, encouraged by the prophetess Deborah to take the lead in the struggle against the Canaanites, seized Mount Tabor with 10,000 men and, rushing down the mountain, defeated Sisera's army at its foot and along the right bank of the Kishon, near Megiddo. A splendid "song of Deborah and Barak" celebrates the victory (Judg 5).

bar'ley

Extensively cultivated in Palestine and neighboring countries from the earliest times.

Bar'na·bas

The surname given by the apostles to Joses or Joseph, a Levite of Cyprus, who was sent by them to Antioch to confirm the church there. From Antioch he "went forth to Tarsus to seek for Saul," whom he had introduced at Jerusalem to Peter and James as a new convert. When he had brought him to Antioch, they remained there together for a year, and "taught much people." Barnabas accompanied Paul on his first missionary journey, and on his journey to the council at Jerusalem, and afterward at Antioch. When Paul, starting on his second missionary journey, refused to take John Mark, the cousin of Barnabas, the two apostles separated, Barnabas taking Mark with him to Cyprus. Paul refers to him in 1 Cor 9.6; Gal 2.13; Col 4.10. The authorship of the Epistle to the Hebrews was attributed to Barnabas by Tertullian. The Codex Sinaiticus includes an "Epistle of

Barnabas," which was regarded as canonical by many in the ancient church, but is held to date from the beginning of the 2nd century A.D. (Acts 4.36, 37; 8.1; 9.1, 27; 11.19-27, 30; 13.2, 3, 9, 13; 14.12, 14; 15).

Bar·thol'o·mew

(Aram. "son of Talmai"). One of the twelve apostles of Jesus (Mt 10.3; Mk 3.18; Lk 6.14; Acts 1.13). He is identified with Nathanael of Cana of Galilee (John 1.45-51; 21.2) on the ground that (1) Bartholomew is not mentioned in John, nor is Nathanael in the other three gospels; and (2) Philip in the first three gospels is associated with Bartholomew, and in John with Nathanael.

Ba'shan

A high tableland, 1600 to 2300 ft., sometimes considered coextensive with the Kingdom of Og.

bat

Classed among unclean winged creatures. It swarms in the numberless ravines, caves, and ruins of Palestine (Lev 11.19; Deut 14.19; Is 2.20).

bay tree

Does not refer to a particular kind of tree, but to a tree growing luxuriantly in its native soil, and is thus translated by the revisers (Ps 37.35). There is no ground for identifying the tree with the bay or noble laurel.

bdel'li·um

What is meant is uncertain, possibly a gem, but some have suggested a vegetable gum, others pearls (Gen 2.12; Num 11.7).

bean

Used both as a vegetable and as flour by the
Jews.

B

bear

The Syrian brown bear was found in the N of
Palestine as recently as the early 20th century.
It is mentioned frequently in the OT.

beard

Full beards were common among Hebrews.
Egyptians and Romans shaved the beard. Assyrians are portrayed with beards. Hebrews were
forbidden to trim the beard; its removal or
plucking was an insult, except in cases of
leprosy.

Ancient types of beards

beat'en oil

Oil produced by crushing fully ripe olives, without pressing, was of the first quality, used for
the lamp of the sanctuary.

bed

The poorer people in Palestine slept upon the bare floor, wrapped in their cloaks, or upon a mattress or quilt, which was rolled up and put away in the daytime. The wealthy used a wooden framework covered with cushions as a divan by day and a bed at night, and the more luxurious had bedsteads carved and inlaid with ivory. The bed of Og (Deut 3.11) was probably a sarcophagus of ironstone.

bee

Canaan was described as a land of milk and honey, which indicates that bees were plentiful. Honey entered into commerce with Tyre (Ezek 27.17).

Be·el′ze·bub, Be·el′ze·bul

The names used by Jesus and others for the chief or prince of devils.

bee′tle

Possibly the long-horned grasshopper.

be·he′moth

(Heb. "dumb beast") A name for the hippopotamus; sometimes, a mythical creature.

Bel

(Akkad. "he who possesses") The state god of Babylon (Marduk).

Be′li·al

(Heb. "worthless, useless") A liar; an iniquitous, wicked person.

Bel·shaz′zar

Babylonian prince, co-regent with his father Nabonidus.

Be·na'iah

(Heb. "Yah has built") The name of 9 persons in the OT, one of whom was a son of Jehaida, a valiant warrior under David, and commander of Solomon's army.

Ben'ja·min

The youngest son of Jacob; Rachel, his mother, died at his birth. Joseph, his brother, demanded that he be brought to Egypt before he would help his brothers. The tribe of Benjamin was the smallest of the tribes.

Ber'o·dach-bal'a·dan

See Merodach-Baladan.

ber'yl

A silicate of beryllium and aluminum; the crystals are usually green. The emerald is of the same type.

Beth'a·ny

A village on the E slope of the Mount of Olives. It is 1⅝ mi. E of Jerusalem, and is now called el-'Aziriyeh.

Beth·az'ma·veth

A town identified with modern Hizmeh, 5 mi. NNE of Jerusalem.

Beth'el

(Heb. "house of God") More frequently mentioned than any city except Jerusalem, Bethel (now Beitin) lies 14 mi. N of Jerusalem. It was founded before 2000 B.C., has been destroyed several times despite being heavily fortified, and has been excavated. Near here Abraham built his altar. The Ark of the Covenant rested here, and the place is associated with Jacob and Eli-

jah and with the tabernacle. Jeroboam made it
a place of idolatry.

Be·thes'da, Beth·za'tha

A spring, possibly with medicinal properties,
near the sheep gate or market in Jerusalem. The
precise location is not now known.

Beth'le·hem

(Heb. "house of bread"?) A very old town,
about 6 mi. SSW of Jerusalem, associated with
David, Ruth, and many other persons of the
OT, and the birthplace of Jesus.

Beth'shan, Beth·she'an

(Heb. "house of safety") A fortress city at the
N end of the Jordan Valley, dating back to the
4th millennium B.C. It was along the route between Egypt, Damascus, and Arabia. Excavations there have provided much information on
life in Bible times.

Beth·she'mesh

(Heb. "house of the seen") The name of 4
places mentioned in the OT, one of which, 24
mi. W of Jerusalem, was first settled in the 3rd
millennium B.C., as shown by excavations there.

Beth-za'tha

See Bethesda.

bier

The Israelites, like the later Jews, buried the
bodies of their dead. The burial was within a
few hours after death. Probably the wooden
framework of a bed served for a bier, as the
same word is used for both.

birds

There are in Palestine about 350 species of birds,

26 of which are peculiar to that country. In the Law, 19 or 20 species of birds, mostly carnivorous, are (with the addition of the bat) declared to be unclean. The birds caught for food were chiefly pigeon, partridge, and quail. The dove is mentioned in the Bible more than 50

Birds perched in a mimosa tree, from an Egyptian wall painting of about the time of Abraham

times, and was the bird with which the Israelites were most familiar. Turtledoves and young pigeons were the only birds used for sacrifices; hence there was a busy trade in them in the neighborhood of the Temple. There are many Scriptural allusions to the habits of pigeons. Dovecots made of pots imbedded in clay are numerous in Palestine. They are often placed inside the walls in the houses of the poor. At the present day partridges abound, and also wild ducks, especially near the Dead Sea. There is, on the whole, a deficiency of singing birds, though blackbirds, larks, finches, cuckoos, and Palestine nightingales are heard in spring. There are many birds of prey.

birth'right

A position of peculiar honor and privilege assigned to the eldest son. The birthright could be parted with or lost through misconduct.

bish'op

(Gr. "overseer") In the NT one of the overseers of a Christian congregation, synonymous with presbyter (elder).

bi·tu'men

("asphalt," "slime") The name includes several compounds of carbon and hydrogen, from which pitch, asphalt, etc., are obtained. Bitumen is often washed up on the shores of the Dead Sea. It is found near Nineveh and at the base of Hermon, and there are springs of it in the Euphrates Valley. This substance is not necessarily connected with volcanic disturbances. Also called *slime*.

boar, wild

Wild boars are especially numerous in the thickets and brakes of the Jordan Valley, whence, when the river rises just before harvest, they are driven out, and play havoc with the cornfields and cultivated ground of the uplands. They are equally common in the southern wilderness, where they plough the ground for the bulbs that abound there.

Bo'az

A virtuous and wealthy man of Bethlehem, who married the widow Ruth of Moab.

Booths, Feast of

An autumn festival, one of the 3 great annual festivals in Israel.

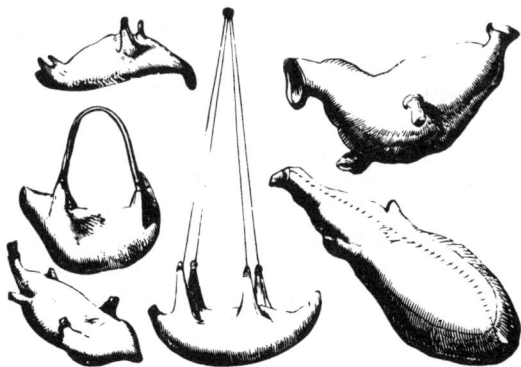

Leather bottles

box

The box shrub has been found in Palestine. *See* Pine.

bram'ble, bri'er, this'tle, thorn

About 20 biblical words imply thorny or spiny flora. Spine-bearing plants form a considerable portion of the flora of Palestine.

brass

Copper alloy. *See* copper.

bread

Commonly of wheat meal, sometimes of barley. The meal was kneaded in wooden troughs; the dough was then mixed with yeast or leaven, pressed or cut into thin, round cakes, then baked over hot stones or in an oven.

breth'ren of Jesus

Four in number (Mt 13.55; Mk 6.3), during His life unbelieving (Jn 7.3-7), were among the earliest members (Acts 1.14) and missionaries (1 Cor. 9.5) of the church. One of them, James the Lord's brother, had the authority of an Apostle (Gal 1.19; 2.9 and 12).

brick

Sun-dried brick made from muddy clay was widely used in the ancient world, but in Babylonia it was kiln dried. Often bricks were stamped with seals or names. Mortar in most areas was the same material as the bricks; in Assyria and Babylonia bitumen was used.

bri'er

See Bramble.

brim'stone

See Sulphur.

broom

A desert shrub.

Babylonian brick

bronze
　Copper alloy. *See* copper.
Bul
　The 8th month in the Hebrew calendar.

bul'rush

The papyrus, which formerly grew in the Nile, rooting itself in the river mud. It is now extinct in Egypt, though still found higher up the Nile valley. It covers acres of the shallow water in Lake Merom. The papyrus has a triangular stem 8 to 10 feet high, terminating in a bush of slender leaves. Paper is made by pressing the pith into sheets.

bur'i·al

Probably, as it now is in Palestine, on the day of death, or next day. As soon as death had taken place, the eyes of the dead were closed. The body was washed, anointed, and swathed in linen. There is no mention of the Egyptian custom of embalming as having ever been followed by Israelites. In OT times the dead appear to have been buried in the clothes worn in life. The dead body was carried to the grave on an open bier, followed by the mourners and professional wailing-women. Burning of the dead was resorted to only in the case of criminals guilty of the most hateful of crimes and was regarded with horror. It was the greatest calamity to be deprived of burial. Many passages of the OT prove the desire of Israelites to be buried in the family burying-place ("with their fathers"), an evidence of their belief that the communion of kindred subsisted after death. The burial places were graves dug in the earth, caves, or chambers hewn in the rock, and closed with large stones to secure them from wild beasts. Such rock sepulchers abound in the neighborhood of Jerusalem. In later times the custom arose of whitewashing every year after the rainy season the stones enclosing the sepulchers, to prevent passersby from being accidentally defiled by touching them.

burnt of'fer·ings

Sacrifices in which the victim was wholly burnt with fire, to express the entire surrender of the offerer to God.

bush, burn'ing

The bush that flamed as the angel called Moses may have been an acacia or a thorn bush. It has not been identified.

C

Caes·a·re'a

A city founded as Straton in the 4th century B.C., on the coast of Palestine 23 mi. S of Mt. Carmel. It was given to Herod by Augustus; Herod renamed it Caesarea in honor of Augustus and rebuilt it as a seaport.

Caes·a·re'a Phi·lip'pi

The name given by Philip the Tetrarch to Paneas, at the main Jordan source, and at the foot of Hermon; now the village of Banias.

Ca'ia·phas

Jewish high priest in the time of Jesus. His proper name was Joseph, Caiaphas being his surname. He was a son-in-law of Annas, high priest (A.D. 7-14). Under the Roman dominion the high priests were frequently changed; but Caiaphas held the office long. He was appointed by Pilate's predecessor, Valerius Gratus, probably about A.D. 18, and not removed till after the deposition of Pilate by Vitellius, governor of Syria, in A.D. 36. The statement (John 11.49; 18.13) that Caiaphas was "high priest that year" has led some to suppose wrongly that the high priests were at that time changed every year. The usage of Josephus in extending the title high priest to all those still living who had held the office explains how Annas is so styled in Acts 4.6 and probably John 18.19, 22.

cal'a·mus

Sweet flag was imported from a far country, possibly India, and sold in the markets of Tyre, and is still brought to the Damascus market from Arabia. Its root stock is aromatic. It was a chief ingredient of the holy anointing oil.

cal'en·dar

The Hebrews early used the equinox as the beginning of the new year, the agricultural year beginning in the spring and the civil or religious year in the autumn. The month was related to the lunar month, and seems to have been counted from the spring new year even when the autumnal new year was used; the use of the lunar month provided only 354¼ days instead of the necessary 365¼ between successive spring equinoxes, so that every few years an extra month had to be provided. The months were first given Canaanite names; then they came to be known by number and eventually, after the Exile, some of the Babylonian names were adopted. Various ways of adjusting the year were suggested by various persons, the added days sometimes early in the year, sometimes late. The 12-month sequence was not otherwise disturbed, and corresponded roughly with our contemporary calendar as follows: *Abib* or *Nisan*, April; *Ziv* or *Iyyar*, May; *Sivan*, June; *Tammuz*, July; *Ab*, August; *Elul*, September; *Ethanim* or *Tishri*, October; *Bul* or *Marchewan*, November; *Chislev*, December; *Tebeth*, January; *Shebat*, February; *Adar*, March.

Cal′va·ry

The place of the Crucifixion. Tradition places it where the Church of the Holy Sepulchre now stands. Other places in Jerusalem have been suggested.

Camels

cam′el

The camel, usually the Arabian, single-humped, has been the beast of burden and means of travel in the Near and Middle East for more than 3 millenniums. There is the slower burden-bearing camel and the swifter dromedary. The two-humped camel appears less often. The camel can go without water for several days, and its flat feet make it capable of traveling over sand. In biblical times, trade caravan travel across the deserts was commonplace; during warfare the camels carried supplies. Camel's milk was used, and the hair was woven into cloth used for tents and coarse robes such as that worn by John the Baptist.

cam'phire, cam'phor
See Henna.

Ca'naan, Ca'naan·ites
(Hurrian? "reeds"? "red purple"?) Canaan included the land between the Jordan River and the sea and the portion of Syria along the coast. The Canaanites were an advanced people, with a written language of 80 characters by 2000 B.C. It was an agricultural society, probably including merchants and seamen. The Hebrews learned writing from them, were sometimes attracted by their gods, intermarried with them, warred with them, and merged with them, seemingly in the 14th century B.C.

can'dle·stick
The candlestick of biblical times is properly called a *lampstand*. Many have been found in excavations. The earliest lamps were pottery saucers of olive oil, into which was laid a twisted thread as a wick. As early as 3000 B.C. the rims were pinched into lips to hold the thread wicks. Herod's temple had a seven-branched lampstand, called the Menorah, with a cup of oil at the top of each branch.

Ca·per'na·um
Excavations have shown Capernaum to be the

The seven-branched candlestick, representing that taken from the temple of Herod in the sack of Jerusalem in A.D. 69-70.

present Tell Hum, on the NNW coast of the Sea of Galilee.

Caph′tor

The traditional homeland of the Philistines; Caphtor has been identified as Crete. It has also been considered possible that the Philistines originated in the Aegean area and had sufficient contact with Cretans to have adopted dress and customs from them.

Cap·pa·do′ci·a

The area W of the Euphrates, S of the Black Sea, N of the Taurus Mountains, E of Galatia.

cap·tiv′i·ty

See Exile.

car′bun·cle

A red stone, garnet or ruby. Error in translation has in a few instances made it a green stone, such as emerald or beryl.

Car′che·mish, Char′che·mish

An ancient and important city on the Euphrates, an objective in warfare between Assyria and Egypt. Excavation has revealed its great antiquity. The present name is Jerablus.

Car′mel

(Heb. "garden," "orchard") A high headland on the coast of Palestine. The modern city of Haifa lies below.

cart

Goods were transported for the most part on the backs of men or of animals; but a cart, probably with 2 solid wheels, was also in use for carrying grain or other produce.

Courtesy of *The Interpreter's
Dictionary of the Bible*

Upper: an ancient Egyptian cart: lower: a cart with
captured women; from Lachish

cas′sia

A coarser kind of cinnamon.

cat

Apparently not commonly known in W Asia in
biblical times. The cat was domesticated in
Egypt 13 centuries before Christ. It was there a

sacred animal, and thousands of mummified cats have been found.

cat′er·pil·lar

(Heb. "to peel off," "finish") Also translated as "destroying locust," "destroyer."

cat′tle

Words meaning cattle appear in the oldest languages. The Hebrews had oxen, asses, horses, sheep, and goats, and were familiar with camels.

ce′dar

Lebanon cedar grows also on the Taurus and Atlas Mountains. It was the king of trees, the symbol of grandeur, might, loftiness, and continuous expansion. Its wood was used in the successive temples at Jerusalem and in the palace of Nebuchadnezzar.

Ce′dron

See Kidron.

Cen′chre·a

Seaport 7 mi. E of Corinth.

chal·ced′o·ny

(Gr. *chalkedon*) One of the many varieties of minutely crystalline silica, of a light, translucent color, related to agate.

Chal·de′a, Chal·dea′a

The plain of Babylon, or lower Mesopotamia; a region of swamps and lakes. One of its great cities was Ur of the Chaldees.

Chal·de′ans

The early people of Chaldea were fishermen and small-scale herdsmen and farmers, opposed to urbanized life. They were not willing to perform any kind of military service and avoided taxes.

They were at times under the control of Babylonia or Assyria; later, Chaldea controlled Babylonia and a wide empire, gradually changing the name from Babylonia to Chaldea. During this period Chaldea assisted in the conquest of Nineveh, the capital of Assyria. Thereafter Chaldea declined, and the Chaldeans went into the world as astrologers, magicians, fortune tellers, and diviners. As such they were famous throughout the Egyptian, Greek, and Roman worlds. The name is still associated with magic.

cha·me′le·on

A lizardlike creature.

cham′ois

A mountain sheep; a small, goat-like antelope.

Char′che·mish

See Carchemish.

char′i·ot

There were disk-wheeled vehicles drawn by asses in the 4th millennium B.C. in Mesopotamia. The first spoked wheels appeared about the time of Hammurabi. The vehicle was two-wheeled, closed in front and open behind, arranged to carry arrows and battle axes, and had a crew of 2, warrior and driver. Usually 2 horses were used. Around 1800 B.C. the chariot was the most powerful of weapons. With it, the Hyksos conquered most of Syria and Egypt. There were also gold and silver chariots and others painted and decorated for pleasure and display by royalty and the wealthy. When the Hebrews first entered Canaan, the Canaanites were using iron chariots; the Hebrews themselves apparently did not have chariots until the time of David. They traded grain to the Egyptians for horses.

Courtesy of *The Interpreter's Dictionary of the Bible*

Assyrian relief of a royal chariot

Ched·or·la·o·mer

An Elamite king with whom Abraham contended.

Che'mosh

God of the Moabites.

che'rub (pl. **cher'u·bim**)

A symbolical winged creature with a human face. Two cherubim were placed on the mercy seat or covering of the Ark of the Covenant in the Tabernacle and in the Temple, and figures representing cherubim were wrought into the hangings of the Holy of Holies.

chest'nut tree

A tall and majestic tree, growing near water in Palestine. From the globular form of the flowers and fruits it is often called button-tree. *See* Plane tree.

Chin'ne·roth, Cin'ne·roth

An early name of the Sea of Galilee. Also the name of a district in Naphtali and of a fortified city in the district, now Tell el-'Oreimeh. Some excavation has been carried on at this site.

Chis'lev

The 9th month in the Hebrew calendar.

Chit'tim, Kit'tim

Greek Kition, the Phoenician port of Cyprus; the modern Larnaka. *See* Cyprus.

Christ

The coming of a Christ (Messiah) was foretold often in the OT, perhaps the most notable prophecy being in Is 9–11. He was to be of the House of David; justice and righteousness never ending would be established on His coming. This was not universally accepted; there were many unbelievers when Jesus was born, who remained unbelievers throughout His life. The believers accepted Him as God the Son, the second member of the Trinity, Christ (meaning the Anointed One), the Messiah, the One foretold: Jesus the Christ, Christ Jesus. His complete acceptance of Himself as the Son of God had its influence in winning many doubters, and the incomparable beauty and power of His preaching influenced constantly increasing numbers of mankind.

Chron'i·cles

The two *Books of Chronicles* have much in common with the books of Samuel and Kings.

They contain genealogical tables from Adam to the death of Saul, the reign of Solomon, the division of the kingdom, the exile, and the proclamation of Cyrus.

chro·nol'o·gy

It is doubtful that the authors of the books of the Bible were in any way conscious of writing history as history is known today. The calendar developed as they developed. They knew seasons rather than days, and periods of war or of peace or succession of rulers rather than years. Consequently a tidy arrangement by years is difficult for either OT or NT. Records of then contemporary governments, which have been and still are being revealed through excavations in the Near and Middle East, are constantly being checked against the gaps and uncertainties of the biblical record. It is possible that in time a complete chronology can be determined.

chrys'o·lite

(Gr. "chrysolithus") Properly this is a greenish-yellow gem, a variety of olivine, a ferromagnesian silicate. In early times the name was usually applied to the Oriental topaz, a yellow variety of corundum.

chrys'o·prase

(Gr. "chrysoprasos") An apple-green variety of chalcedony.

church

(Gr. *Ekklesia,* "an assembly") In the NT it is used in the following senses:

1. An ordinary public meeting (Acts 19.32, 39, 41).

2. The congregation of the Israelites under the Old Testament.

3. A meeting of Christians for worship.

4. The company of Christians associated for the worship and service of God in a particular locality or region.

5. The whole body of Christians throughout the world.

6. In the widest sense, the whole body of the redeemed.

Cin'ner·roth

See Chinneroth.

cir·cum·cis'ion

Removal of the foreskin. Circumcision was widely practiced; of the neighbors of the Hebrews, only the Philistines did not practice it.

cith'ern

A lyre-like instrument with 11 or 12 strings.

cit'ies

There were many ancient cities. Carbon-14 dating shows a wall and fortification at Jericho before 7000 or 8000 B.C. Cities had surrounding villages, whose inhabitants went inside the city walls in times of danger. The population of Ur of the Chaldees, where Abraham was born, has been estimated at a quarter to a half million.

cit'y of ref'uge

Crimes of violence were in ancient civilizations often avenged by the injured person himself or by a relative. But the accused person could be sure of trial according to the laws of the time and country if he could get to a city of refuge. In Palestine there were 6, 3 of them across the

Jordan. The cities in Canaan were Kedesh,
Shechem, and Hebron. The trans-Jordan cities
were Bezer, Ramoth-Gilead, and Golan. Biblical
law restricted refuge to the accidental homicide.

cloke, cloak

Originally a long strip of coarse cloth thrown
over the shoulders. Later it became elaborated,
of finer material, fitted, even embroidered. A
creditor might seize this garment, but not the
inner one. Sometimes called a *robe*, a *mantle*,
a *garment*.

cloud

See Pillar of cloud and of fire.

coat

A garment worn under the mantle, usually tied
by a girdle.

coat of mail

A sleeveless armor made (1) of skin or leather;
or (2) of small plates of bronze or iron, sewn
on leather or fastened together in rows.

coins

See Money.

Co·los'si·ans

The Letter (Epistle) of Paul to the Colossians
was written by Paul, while he was a prisoner in
Rome, to the Christians at Colossae in Asia
Minor. Paul writes to encourage them with real
truth—that through Christ they have the everlasting love of God.

com'fort·er

A paraclete. One who stands by to aid, to
counsel, to strengthen; an advocate.

com·mand'ments
See Ten Commandments.

co'ney
(Heb. "the hider") A small animal, sometimes called a rock rabbit or rock badger. It is forbidden as food.

C

cop'per, brass, bronze
The name copper derives ultimately from Cyprus, the famous copper source of the ancient world. Egyptians, Edomites, and others mined copper in the Arabah, the area between the Dead Sea and the Gulf of Aqabah; Solomon's copper mines have been identified. Some articles made of copper have been found in excavations in the Holy Land. More bronze articles have been found; bronze is an alloy of copper and tin. The Phoenicians brought in tin ore as an article of commerce, and the Hebrews knew smelting and metallurgy. Brass, made of copper and zinc, has not been found, and seems not to have been made, nor have zinc deposits or worked-out mines been found.

cor'al
The red coral of the Mediterranean, used for beads and ornaments, was an article of commerce, and was considered a precious stone.

cor'ban
A Hebrew word, which is translated "offering" or "oblation," hence referring to any article or possession solemnly dedicated to God. Our Lord rebuked those who adopted this device to escape the necessity of supporting their parents.

co·ri·an'der
An annual plant, with seeds used as a spice.

Cor'inth
A city of Southern Greece, 40 mi. SW of Athens. Cenchreae was its eastern harbor. Destroyed by the Romans in 146 B.C., it was rebuilt by Julius Caesar in 46 B.C., and peopled by a colony of veterans and others. Situated on the isthmus which had always formed the highway of commerce between Asia and Italy, it became the metropolis of the Roman province of Achaia, the meeting-place of all the social forces of the age, and a center of licentiousness, much of it in the form of pagan religion and rites. The city was the home of Aquila and Priscilla, who became great friends of Paul and his assistants in evangelism in both Corinth and Ephesus; Paul was their frequent visitor.

Co·rin'thi·ans
The *Letters of Paul to the Corinthians* were written from Ephesus about 57 A.D. The Christians of Corinth found it hard to live as they knew they should and questioned Paul about their difficulties. In *First Corinthians* Paul answers their question, points out to them what they have done wrong, and encourages them with his message. "You are Christ's." *Second Corinthians* contains Paul's message of thanksgiving and love. Then he goes on to describe his tribulations as he went about preaching the gospel of Christ.

cor'mo·rant
A bird not positively identified.

corn

This is a general term, meaning grain. The grains grown in Palestine are wheat, barley, millet, and spelt. *See* Wheat.

cor′net

(Lat. *cornu*) A horn, a wind instrument made of horn, wood, or metal.

cos·met′ics

Ointments were used to counteract the dry heat of the climate, and perfumes were added to the ointments. Eye paint, usually black, was also used, and there is doubtful reference to henna, used in some cultures not only as a perfume but as a dye for hair, palms, soles of the feet, and nails.

cot′ton, hang′ings, net′work

Cotton was used in the Middle East from very early times. It is probable that the colored hangings in the palace of Susa (Esther 1.6) and the networks woven in Egypt (Is 19.9) were of cotton.

court

See Temple.

cov′e·nant

The religion of Israel rested on a covenant between Jehovah and that people. God founded the covenant by His promise, and His people's part in it was the fulfillment of the divine command. Entrance into it was marked by the sign of circumcision. A New Covenant was promised by the prophets; and this is established in Christ.

Cov′e·nant, Ark of the

See Ark of the Covenant.

Cov′e·nant, the Book of the

This is taken to refer to Ex 20.23–23.33.

crafts, crafts′men

Many craftsmen worked in their homes or had shops; sometimes a single craft occupied a special area in a town. Their number and diversity were increased notably by contact with the Canaanites and with the Babylonians during the Exile. Crafts included boatbuilders, netmakers, carpenters, wood carvers, furniture makers, carvers of ivory and alabaster, weavers, tanners, goldsmiths, silversmiths, bronzesmiths, leatherworkers, tentmakers, carpetmakers, ropemakers, basketmakers, fullers, dyers, jewelers, glassworkers, lampmakers, potters.

cre·a′tion

Cuneiform tablets have been discovered that give the different accounts of the creation current in Babylonia. One of them, in the form of a long poem, resembles in many respects the account in Gen 1. It commences with the statement that "in the beginning" all was chaos of waters. Then the Upper and Lower Firmaments were created, and the gods came into existence. After that comes a long account of the struggle between Bel-Marduk and the "Dragon" of Chaos, "the serpent of evil," with her allies, the forces of anarchy and darkness. It ended in the victory of the god of light, who thereupon created the present world by the power of his "word." The fifth tablet or book of the poem describes the appointment of the heavenly bodies for signs and seasons, and the sixth (or perhaps the seventh) the creation of animals and reptiles.

Crete
An island in the Mediterranean SE of Greece. Center of Minoan civilization in the time of Abraham. Paul passed along the coast on his way to Rome. There was a Jewish colony on Crete; a Christian group was also established there. The people of the island were not well regarded (Tit 1.12).

crick'et
This may be the long-horned grasshopper.

crim'son, scar'let
Red coloring matter of many shades, extracted from cochineal insects; used for dyeing.

cross
The cross as a means of inflicting death in the most cruel and shameful way was used by the

Crosses

Phoenicians, from whom it passed to the Greeks and the Romans. It consisted of two beams of wood nailed one to the other in the form of X, or T, or +. The last, which is most familiar to us in art, was in all probability the shape of Christ's cross.

cu′cum·ber

Long cultivated in Syria and Egypt.

cum′min

The aromatic seed of an umbelliferous plant, used as a condiment.

curse

In the ancient warfare of the Israelites, as of the neighboring nations, the enemy and all his belongings were placed under a ban or curse. Thus on the Moabite stone we read, "I destroyed all the people of the city to delight the eyes of Chemosh and Moab."

Cush, Cu′shan, Cu′san

1. The Cushites in Ethiopia, the Kassites of Babylonia, or a Midianite tribe near Edom.

2. A king of Aram.

cut′ter

See Locust.

cym′bals

These were used in pairs, only by men, as signaling instruments and as accompaniments to the trumpet and lyre.

cy′press

The Hebrew word has been variously translated as pine or larch, box (box shrub), or holm (a form of oak; holly). *See* Holm tree; Pine.

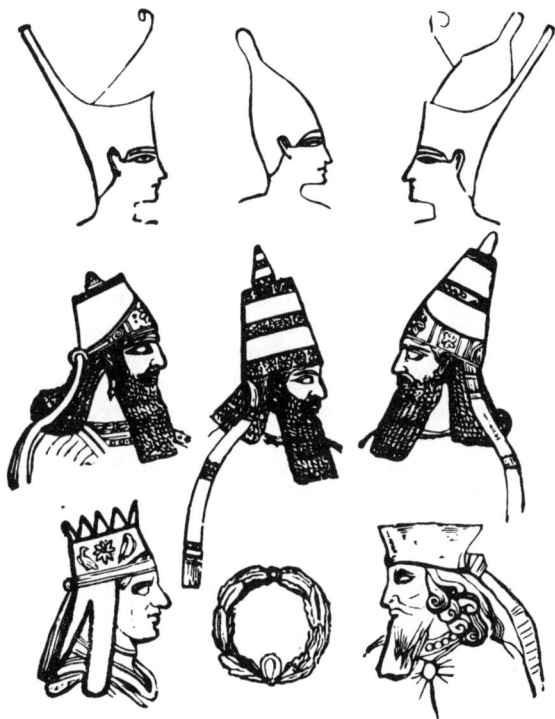

Ancient crowns

Cy′prus
A large island in the Mediterranean, 41 mi. from
the Coast of Asia Minor and 60 mi. from Syria,
also called Chittim or Kittim. In ancient times it
was famous as a source of copper, and a particular pottery made there has been found in widely

scattered excavations. It was the home of Barnabas, and was visited by Paul.

Cy'rus

A Persian king, founder of the Achaemenian dynasty.

D

Da·mas'cus

The first mention of Damascus in an inscription is dated in the 16th century B.C. It claims to be the oldest continuously occupied city site in the world, and is now the capital of Syria. In ancient times it was a widely known caravan center. The city was captured and plundered many times, by Assyria, Babylonia, David of Israel, Persia, Alexander the Great, and Rome.

Dan

1. The fifth son of Jacob.

2. A city in the N of Palestine, identified with Tell el-Qadi, to which the Danites migrated. Jeroboam established idolatry there.

Dan'iel

(Heb. "God has judged") The name of 3 persons in the OT, one of whom is the author of the 4th of the prophetic books. He was taken as a captive to Babylon, where he was trained in the king's palace. Among other triumphs he interpreted the king's dreams and the handwriting on the wall, looked after his own friends, Shadrach, Meshach, and Abednego, and then was cast into a den of lions for refusing to acknowledge Darius the Mede as a god. He was saved by God, and subsequently Darius made him a governor of a province.

Dan'iel, the Book of

The OT book of Daniel is divided into two parts. The first six chapters tell of Daniel's faith and the greatness of his God over the idols of Babylon. The last six chapters contain the four visions of Daniel and their interpretations.

dar'ic

See Money.

Da·ri'us

Darius I and Darius II, rulers of Persia.

Da'vid

(Heb. "beloved") The second and greatest king over Israel, was the youngest son of Jesse, and was born at Bethlehem, where his early youth was spent as a shepherd. While still a stripling he slew the Philistine giant Goliath, and was admitted to the court and service of King Saul, whose melancholy he soothed by his skilful playing on the harp. Saul's daughter Michal became his wife, and Saul's son Jonathan was united to him in a lifelong friendship. Fleeing from the deadly jealously of Saul, he first escaped to the country of the Philistines. Then, gathering at the cave of Adullam a band of 400 (afterward 600) men, he contrived to avoid Saul by moving hither and thither in the S country. For 16 months he lived at Ziklag, as a vassal of the king of Gath. After the death of Saul and Jonathan at Gilboa, David reigned over Judah at Hebron for 7½ years, and after the death of Saul's son Ishbosheth he became king over all Israel. He took the stronghold Jebus, on the hill of Zion (the "city of David"), from the Jebusites, and built a palace there, with a tent beside it, in which the Ark of the Covenant was placed until a temple should be built for it by his successor. In addition to his old guard of 600 gibborim (or "heroes"), now largely recruited from foreigners, especially "Cherethites and Pelethites" (most probably Cretans and Philistines), he had, according to Chronicles, 288,000 fighting men, of whom 24,000 were under arms each month in the year. Several years of successful war made David master of the whole territory from the Euphrates to the Egyptian frontier. In the latter part of his reign of 32 years in Jerusalem, his favorite son Absalom rebelled against him and was slain, to his father's great sorrow; and shortly before his death, which has been variously dated 1015, 980, and 977 B.C., another son, Adonijah, attempted by means of a revolt to frustrate his father's choice of Solomon as successor.

David, while he was the hero of the people, refused to lift his hand against "the Lord's anointed," even in his own defense, contenting himself with an appeal to the Divine judgment. In contrast to Saul, he is "the man after God's own heart." Heroic confidence in God sustained him in all the difficulties of his life and of his reign. "He executed judgment and justice unto all his people," and established the monarchy on a sound civil and religious basis. The greatest

stain upon his character was his foul wrong
done to Uriah, whose wife he wanted, followed
by his indirect murder, by sending him into battle and arranging to have him deserted, sins of
which he bitterly repented. The last song of
"the sweet psalmist of Israel" expresses the
spirit of his life and of his rule. In the darkest
days of the nation's history, men felt that the
promises of God could only be fulfilled under
another David. The memory of the "sure mercies
of David" and the "everlasting covenant" God
made with him quickened their Messianic hope
of One who should be given "for a witness to the
people, a leader and commander to the people."

day

The word may mean the time from sunrise to
sunset; or the civil day of 24 hours, from sunrise to sunrise or from sunset to sunset; or in a
poetic sense of "in the time of" as in the phrase
"in the day of . . ."

Day of A·tone'ment

See Atonement, Day of.

day star, the morning star

The "prophetic word" in 2 Pet 1.19.

dea'con

(Gr. "servant") In the NT, the name of a class
of congregational office-bearers, first mentioned
about A.D. 63. Their work seems chiefly to have
been the visiting and relief of the poor. The
early church appointed 7 in every church, and
assigned to them the special care of the sick
and of the poor.

dea'con·ess, serv'ant

Women especially charged with the care of the poor and sick women. Widows may have constituted a special case.

Dead Sea

This body of water at the mouth of the Jordan River is called in the Bible the Salt Sea, the Sea of the Arabah, the Sea of the Plain. It is about 53 mi. long and 10 mi. wide, 1500 ft. deep, and its surface is 1292 ft. below sea level. It is about 25 per cent salt, 5 times as salty as the ocean. Its mineral compounds are chlorides of magnesium, sodium, calcium, and potassium, as well as magnesium bromide.

Deb'o·rah

1. Rebekah's nurse and her lifelong companion.

2. An early judge of Israel. She roused opposition to Canaanite oppression of Israel, and Judg 5.2-31 is her Song of Victory over Canaan. It is one of the oldest Hebrew poems in existence, dating from the 12th century B.C., and it has been described as one of the most magnificent.

De·cap'o·lis

A federation of 10 Greek cities in Palestine, some of which lay along the trade routes of the day, and several of which were founded by soldiers from the armies of Alexander the Great. Most of them have been identified, and some have been extensively excavated.

Ded·i·ca'tion, Feast of

The principal feast of Dedication was that of the reconsecration of the temple after its desecration by the Greeks, an 8-day celebration today called Hanukkah, in mid-December. Sometimes it is called the Feast of Lights.

De·grees', Songs of, or As·cents', Songs of

The titles of 15 psalms. The degrees or ascents are believed to be the steps between the men's and women's courts of the temple. The Levites stood on these steps to sing these psalms.

D

De·li'lah

Samson's beloved. She was bribed by the Philistines to get for them the secret of his strength, which she did.

del'uge

See flood.

De·struc'tion, Cit'y of

See City of the Sun.

Deu·ter·on'o·my

A sequel to Numbers. Narrated in it are three speeches and two poems, supposedly spoken by Moses in Moab before the crossing of Jordan, in which he gives the Ten Commandments to the chosen people. A minor narrative in three of the chapters tells of the last days of Moses.

Di·a'na of the E·phe'si·ans

This is the Latin name of the ancient goddess of the region of Ephesus; some 300 years after the first Greek settlers had arrived in the area they had adopted this local mother-goddess or fertility goddess as their own, calling her Artemis. By 800 B.C., they had begun to build a magnificent temple for her. Worship of her was widespread and conducted in magnificent rituals and surroundings. The primary image, probably a meteorite, is believed to have been placed in the temple at Ephesus.

Di·as'po·ra, Dis·per'sion

At the time of the Exile the Jewish people scattered widely and settled permanently in Mesopotamia, particularly in Babylonia, and in Alexandria, Asia Minor, and as far away as Cyrenaica.

Di'bon

A Moabite city 13 mi. E of the Dead Sea, 3 mi. N of the Arnon River. The famous Moabite Stone was found in Dibon. It tells of a Moabite victory over Israel at the time of Omri.

dill

Both the plant and the seeds are used as flavoring and have some use in medicine.

Dis·per'sion

See Diaspora.

di·vorce'

The Hebrew name for husband, baal, meant "owner," and in primitive Israel dissolution of marriage might take place at the husband's will. The Book of the Covenant shows that the wife so put away retained the right to be fed and clothed by the husband (Ex. 21.7-11), unless she was redeemed by her own relatives, and thus set free to marry another man. In Deut. 24.1–4 it is enacted that the husband must give a dismissed wife a "bill of divorcement," a document releasing her from all claims on his part and setting her free to marry again.

Our Lord teaches that marriage rests on the original creative ordinance of God, making the bond between man and wife indissoluble, and that the Mosaic legislation with regard to divorce was a concession to natural hardness of heart, and did not correspond to its divine idea (Mt 19.4-9; 5.31 ff). Divorce was permissible only in the case of unfaithfulness (Mt 5.32; 19.9).

dog

Mentioned about 40 times in Scripture, almost always in a tone of contempt. The Jews, not being a hunting people, did not train the dog, except to guard their flocks (Job 30.1). They had not the noble mastiffs and wolfhounds we find carved on Assyrian monuments, nor the varied breeds of hunting dogs portrayed on the Egyptian walls. Their dogs were, doubtless, as they are still in Palestine, pariah or ownerless dogs, of a type not unlike the Scottish collie. Their nocturnal habits are referred to in Ps 59.14, 15. In the East they are the scavengers of the towns. The term dog is still hurled in reproach by the Jew at the Gentile and by the Moslem at the Christian. Christians also use it.

Do'than

The place where Joseph found his brothers. Now called Tell Dotha, excavations show it to have been a city from about 3000 B.C. to A.D. 300 or 400.

drach'ma

The unit of silver coinage of Greece; spoken of as a piece of silver.

drag'on

This seems to have been a fabulous monster of tremendous strength. It is called leviathan, sea monster, Rahab (in poetic passages only) and sea serpent. *See* Whale.

dress

The outermost garment of men may have been a rectangular piece of cloth, a mantle, cloak, cloke, wrapped about the body. Under that was a garment called a coat, tunic, robe or chiton (Greek), which might have been baglike, with openings for arms and head and of various lengths. A loincloth or girdle might be worn; the priests had breeches. The girdle and the tunic might be made of skins of animals. Cloth woven of wool, linen, animal hair, or fine linen (probably cotton) was used, of varying degrees of beauty and elegance. The draped or wrapped garments were tied around by a girdle, a long folded wool cloth, through which a sword might be thrust; also, it might be folded in such a way as to provide a money belt. Sandals were worn, fastened by leather straps. Men of importance wore a ring or rings. There was elaborate jewelry for men of rank or wealth. Women's clothing was similar, sometimes more elaborate, being decorated with fringe or other ornamentation. Women had more head dresses, veils, and ornaments than men. A number of dyes were used.

drom'e·da·ry

A finer and swifter race of camel, differing from the ordinary camel as a race horse does from a cart horse. According to an Arabic proverb, "Men are like camels—not one in a hundred is a dromedary."

E

ea′gle, gier, vul′ture

The largest flying birds of Palestine, all unclean for food. The vulture is a carrion-eating bird. The same Heb. word has been thus variously translated.

ear of grain

The individual head of grain.

ear′ring

These ornaments seem usually to have been circular in shape, made of gold. Men may have worn a single earring.

E′bal

A mountain N of Mount Gerizim and forming the N side of an E to W pass with Gerizim on the S.

eb′on·y

The core wood of several varieties of ebony, imported from Ceylon, S India, and possibly from Ethiopia. Egyptians, Babylonians, Greeks, Romans, and Phoenicians made furniture of ebony inlaid with ivory. Idols were also carved from ebony.

Ec·cle·si·as′tes

The book of *Ecclesiastes* contains the writings of a wealthy Jew who suffered from the sorrows and disappointments of life and now tries to discover the true value and meaning of life through God. The author of this book calls himself "The Preacher," "The son of David," and "king in Jerusalem." But whether this was Solomon or a later "son of David" is uncertain.

E'den

The root of the Hebrew word is uncertain, and the location of Eden has not been determined. The plain of the Tigris-Euphrates rivers has been most favored.

E'dom

(Heb. "the red region") Edom extended from the Brook Zered about 70 mi. toward the Gulf of Aqabah, with an approximate 15-mi. width. Excavations show a busy civilization there between the 23rd and 20th centuries, after which the only inhabitants were wandering Bedouins. In the 13th century the Edomites, a Semitic people, arrived. They were at war much of the time with the Israelites; David conquered them, making possible trade with Arabia and access to the copper mines of Edom. Later, Amaziah and his successor Azariah again conquered the country. After the Exile, the Edomites moved into Palestine. Eventually, Rome conquered the entire area.

E'gypt

The name applied since the time of Homer to the land of the Nile, in the NE of Africa. Egypt consists geographically of 2 halves, the N being the Delta, and the S, Upper Egypt, between Cairo and the First Cataract. The Hebrews called it Mizraim, the land of Ham, or Rahab. The Egyptians belonged to the Mediterranean race and their original home is still a matter of dispute. The ancient Egyptian language, of which the latest form is Coptic, is distantly connected with the Semitic family of speech.

The civilization of Egypt goes back to a remote antiquity. The two kingdoms, the north and the south, were united by Menes, founder of the first historical dynasty of kings. The first 6 dynasties, lasting until 2200 B.C., constitute what is known as the Old Kingdom, which had its capital at Memphis, S of Cairo (the Old Testament Moph or Noph). The native name was Mennofer, "the good place." The Pyramids were tombs of the monarchs of the Old Kingdom, those of Gizeh being erected in the time of the Fourth Dynasty.

After the fall of the Old Kingdom came a period of decline and obscurity, followed by the Middle Kingdom, the most powerful dynasty of which was the Twelfth. The Faiyum was rescued for agriculture by the kings of the Twelfth Dynasty, and 2 obelisks were erected in front of the temple of the Sun-god at On or Heliopolis (near Cairo), one of which is still standing. The capital of the Middle Kingdom was Thebes, in Upper Egypt.

The Middle Kingdom was overthrown by the Hyksos (*haq schas,* Bedouin chieftains) or Shepherd princes from Asia, whose three dynasties ruled over Northern Egypt for several centuries. They had their capital at Zoan or Tunis (now San), in the NE part of the Delta. In their time Abraham, Jacob, and Joseph entered Egypt. The Hyksos were finally expelled about 1600 B.C. by the hereditary princes of Thebes, who founded the Eighteenth Dynasty, and carried the war into Asia. Canaan, Syria, and Cyprus were subdued, and the boundaries of the Egyptian Kingdom were fixed at the Euphrates. The Sudan, which had been conquered by the kings of the Twelfth Dynasty, was again annexed to Egypt, and the eldest son of the Pharaoh took the title of prince of Cush. One of the later kings of the dynasty, Amen-hotep IV (1369-1353 B.C.), taking the name Akh-en-Aton (spirit of the sun), endeavored to supplant the ancient state religion of Egypt by a pantheistic monotheism derived from Asia, the one supreme god being adored under the image of the solar disk. The attempt led to religious and civil war, and the Pharaoh retreated from Thebes to Central Egypt, where he built a new capital, on the site of the present Tel el-Amarna. The cuneiform tablets that were found here in 1887 represent his foreign correspondence. He surrounded himself with officials and courtiers of Asiatic and more especially Canaanitish extraction; but the native party succeeded eventually in overthrowing the government; the capital of Amenhotep was destroyed, and the foreigners were driven out of the country—those that remained being reduced to serfdom.

The national triumph was marked by the rise of the Nineteenth Dynasty, in the founder of which, Ramses I, we must see the "new king, who knew not Joseph." His grandson, Ramses II. reigned 67 years (1290-1224 B.C.), and was an indefatigable builder. Pithom, excavated by Naville in 1883, was one of the cities he built; he may have been the Pharaoh of the Oppres-

Egyptian standards

sion. The Pharaoh of the Exodus may have been one of his immediate successors, whose reigns were short. Under them Egypt lost its empire in Asia, and was itself attacked by barbarians from Libya and the north.

The Nineteenth Dynasty soon afterward came to an end, Egypt was distracted by civil war, and for a short time a Syrian, Irsu, ruled over it.

Then came the Twentieth Dynasty, the 2nd Pharaoh of which, Ramses III (1195-1164 B.C.), restored the power of his country. In one of his campaigns he overran the S part of Palestine, where the Israelites had not yet settled. They must at the time have been still in the wilderness. But it was during the reign of Ramses III that Egypt finally lost Gaza and the adjoining cities to the Philistines.

After Ramses III, Egypt fell into decay. Solomon married the daughter of one of the last kings of the Twenty-first Dynasty, which was overthrown by Sheshonk or Shishak I, the general of the Libyan mercenaries, who founded the Twenty-second Dynasty (940-745 B.C.). A list of the places he captured in Palestine is engraved on the outside of the S wall of the temple of Karnak.

In the age of Hezekiah, Egypt was conquered by Ethiopians from the Sudan, who constituted the Twenty-fifth Dynasty. The 3rd of them was Tirhakah (689-664 B.C.). In 671 B.C. it was conquered by the Assyrians, who divided it into 20 satrapies, and Tirhakah was driven back to his ancestral dominions. Fourteen years later it successfully revolted under Psamtik or Psammetichus I (663-609 B.C.) of Sais, the founder of the Twenty-sixth Dynasty. Among his successors were Neco of Necho and Hophra, or Apries. The dynasty came to an end in 525 B.C. when the country was subjugated by Cambyses. Soon afterward it became a Persian satrapy.

The title of Pharaoh, given to the Egyptian king, is the Egyptian for Great House. The name is found in very early Egyptian texts.

Egyptian religion was a strange mixture of

pantheism and animal worship, the gods being adored in the form of animals. While the educated classes resolved their many deities into manifestations of one omnipresent and omnipotent divine power, the lower classes regarded the animals as incarnations of the gods. Under the Old Kingdom, Ptah, the Creator, the god of Memphis, was at the head of the Pantheon; afterward Amon, the god of Thebes, took his place. Amon, like most of the other gods, was identified with Re, the sun god of Heliopolis.

The Egyptians believed in a resurrection and a future state of rewards and punishments. The judge of the dead was Osiris, who had been slain by Set, the representative of evil, and afterward restored to life. His death was avenged by his son Horus, whom the Egyptians invoked as their Redeemer. Osiris and Horus, along with Isis, formed a trinity, representing the sun god under different forms.

The Pyramids, the temples, and the obelisks of Egypt have been described in all ages, but it was not until early in the 19th century, through the finding of the Rosetta stone, that the key to reading the hieroglyphic texts was discovered by the French scholar Champollion. The work of Brugsch and Birch then led to the recovery of history contained on the monuments or in papyri. The exacavations of Mariette followed; and those of Petrie and De Morgan further increased our information about the religion, social customs, and history of Egypt. In 1896, among the ruins of a temple of Mer-ne-Ptah at

Thebes, Petrie found a large granite stele, on which is engraved a hymn of victory commemorating the defeat of Libyan invaders who had overrun the Delta. At the end other victories of Mer-ne-Ptah are glanced at, and it is said that "the Israelites (I-s-y-r-a-e-l-u) are minished (?) so that they have no seed." This statement of an egyptian poet is a remarkable parallel to Ex 1.10-22.

E'lah, Val'ley of

(Heb. "valley of the terebinth"?) A valley identified as Wadi es-Sant, 14 mi. WSW of Bethlehem.

E'lam, E'lam·ites

Elam occupied the area of the Zagros Mountains and present-day Luristan and Khuzistan. Its capital was Susa. Its history through about 2 millennia was warfare first with Sumer and subsequently with Babylonia and Assyria. Darius completed the conquest of the country.

el'ders, an'cients

Heads of families and tribes, among the early Hebrews as among other primitive peoples, administered justice within their own circles in time of peace and were the leaders in time of war (cf. the Arabian sheikh, or elder). The "elders of the city" afterward took the place of the elders of tribes and families, retaining their judicial functions. The "judges" and "officers" were probably those among the elders who acted respectively as administrators and executors of justice. When the synagogue became an established institution, the elders who were the civil authorities of a place were also the elders of its synagogue.

The elders or presbyters (Gr. "elders") of Christian churches were local overseers chosen after the model of the synagogue. They appear from the first to have been elected by the people, and, on their being approved by the apostles, to have been instituted to their office by prayer and the laying on of hands. Their duties were to exercise spiritual oversight over the people as pastors, visiting the sick and caring for the poor and for strangers, to maintain order in the religious assemblies, to teach, and to administer the affairs of the congregation, in concurrence with the deacons. The word elder or presbyter was interchangeable with the word bishop in NT times, and the offices were one and the same till about A.D. 150, when the presbyters first became subordinate to the bishops.

el′e·phant

The elephant is not mentioned in the OT, but Solomon imported ivory (1 Kings 10.22; 2 Chron 9.21) so there must have been knowledge of the animal. The Persians used elephants in warfare in the 4th century B.C., and they were used in war against Palestine by the Seleucids in 163 B.C.

E′li

(Heb. "exalted") A judge in Israel, he held that office and the high-priesthood for 40 years at Shiloh. His sons, Hophni and Phinehas, through gross misconduct, disgraced their priestly descent and position; and a great defeat, in which they and many Israelites were slain by the Philistines and the Ark of the Covenant was captured, was regarded as a divine judgment. Eli died of horror at the news and was succeeded by Samuel (1 Sam 1–4).

E·li'hu

(Heb. "he is my God") The name of 5 persons in the OT, one of whom argued with Job and his friends (Job 32–37).

E·li'jah, E·li'as

(Heb. "Yah is God") Elijah the Tishbite was of the inhabitants or sojourners of Gilead. His prophetic ministry belongs to the Northern Kingdom, in the reigns of Ahab and Ahaziah. When Ahab, under the influence of his Tyrian wife Jezebel, threatened to suppress the worship of Jehovah, and made Baal worship the court religion, Elijah suddenly appeared before the king to announce a long drought, in punishment of the apostasy of the covenant nation. While this lasted (3 years) he was at first miraculously fed by ravens at the brook Cherith and afterward lived at Zarephath, a Tyrian city, in the house of a widow, whose son he restored to life. Elijah now appears before Ahab, and challenges the prophets of Baal to a contest between Baal and Jehovah, in which it shall be shown by fire from heaven which is the true God. The fire consumes the sacrifice and altar of Jehovah; the people acknowledge that Jehovah is God, and fall upon the priests of Baal and slay them; and before evening there is a tempest of rain. But this victory is soon followed by defeat; and, despairing of man, Elijah journeys to Horeb to meet God. There a vision passes before him, and reveals to him that God establishes His kingdom not by the violence of earthquake and tempest, but in gentleness and stillness. He returns with new faith to carry out God's commands, on his way to Damascus anointing Elisha to be his successor. Elijah again met Ahab to announce the ruin of his house for his heartless robbery of Naboth, whose death had been compassed by Jezebel. Wonderful as Elijah's whole career was, its completion in which the Enoch miracle was repeated was its most remarkable event. There appeared chariots of fire and horses of fire, and Elijah was taken up to heaven in a whirlwind. Elijah was the leader of the reaction of spiritual religion of Jehovah against the nature religion of Baal, and through his efforts Baal worship was effectually checked in Israel. He was held in high esteem by the later Jews. No other prophet is so often mentioned in the NT. The last prophet, Malachi, prophesies his return before the day of the Lord. This prophecy was literally interpreted in Israel. The evangelists and Jesus show that it was fulfilled in John the Baptist. In the transfiguration of our Lord, Elijah appears as the representative of the prophets, beside Moses, the representative of the law (1 Kings 17–19, 21; 2 Kings 1, 2).

E·li′phaz

(Heb. "God crushes"?) One of Job's friends.

E·li′sha

(Heb. "God is salvation") The son of Shaphat of

Abel-Meholah, Elisha was the disciple and successor of Elijah, to whom he is related much as Joshua is to Moses. His prophetic work belonged to the reigns of Jehoram, Jehu, and Jehoahaz. As the spiritual guide of the people, he showed the same spirit of opposition to the idolatrous court and priesthood that had inspired Elijah, and was to the faithful servants of Jehovah what his great teacher had been before him, "the chariot of Israel, and the horsemen thereof," Israel's strength and protection. Many miracles are recorded as having been wrought by him. He died early in the reign of Joash, at an extreme old age (2 Kings 2-9, 12).

elm
An erroneous translation of ela (Hos 4.13), elsewhere rendered oak, teil tree, or terebinth. The elm is not found in Palestine.

E'lul
The 6th month in the Hebrew calendar.

em·balm'ing
A mode of preserving a dead body from decay by the use of aromatic spices. The art was practiced by the Egyptians from the very earliest times, and was by them brought to great perfection. It probably originated in the belief in the future reunion of the soul and the body. It was rarely practiced by the Jews. The Jewish process required 40 days, and that of the Egyptians 70 days. An embalmed body is a mummy.

em'er·ald
A variety of beryl of rich green color.

Em·ma′us

(Gr. "warm wells") A Judean town, not definitely identified. Four modern towns have been suggested.

En′dor

(Heb. "spring of *dor*") A city in Manasseh, home of a medium or witch consulted by King Saul. Near Endor, Sisera and Jabin were destroyed. Located at the modern Endor.

En·ro′gel

(Heb. "spring of the fuller") A spring in the valley of the Kidron, near Jerusalem.

E·phe′sians

The Letter of Paul to the Ephesians, written about A.D. 62, seems to be a general letter to the churches of Asia Minor. Paul presents God's eternal purpose to save men through faith in Christ; "the dividing wall of hostility" between Jews and Gentiles has been broken down through the cross of Christ. Paul exhorts us to live as worthy, true Christians.

Eph′e·sus

A famous city of Lydia, in Asia Minor, and the capital of Proconsular Asia, it is noted for its Temple of Artemis or Diana and its great theater. It was visited by Paul in his second journey when he left Aquila and Priscilla there to carry on the work; and in his third journey, when Demetrius raised an uproar against him.

eph′od

A priestly garment.

E′phra·im

(Heb. "fruitful") The most powerful of the

tribes of Northern Israel, extended from Benjamin to Manasseh W of Jordan.

E'phra·im, Mount
The tribe of Ephraim lived in hill country; Joshua (an Ephraimite) was buried on Mount Ephraim, but which hill is intended is not known.

E·sar·had'don
King of Assyria and Babylonia (681-669 B.C.).

Es·dra·e'lon
Greek name for the W portion of the Valley of Jezreel, including the Valley of Megiddo. It is a well-watered and fertile valley, which separates Galilee from Samaria. The River Kishon drains it.

Es'dras, First and Sec'ond Books of
In the Vulgate these books appear as 3 and 4 Esdras, because Ezra and Neh have been counted as two books of Ezra. Counting them in this way, *Third Esdras* is a new version of the events relating to the return from the Captivity, the chief incident being a contest before the king by the young wits of the court. Zerubbabel wins with the well-known maxim, *Magna est veritas, et praevalebit,* "Truth is great, and will prevail." In consequence, he obtains concessions for the Jewish captives.

Fourth Esdras has perished in the Greek but is extant in other versions. Its major part is a series of revelations to Ezra regarding the fortunes of Israel and of Jerusalem. Its date is probably after A.D. 70.

Es·senes'

An ascetic order, known to have existed from about 150 B.C. In the time of our Lord they were settled in monastic communities near the Dead Sea and in villages throughout the country. The Dead Sea Scrolls (found in 1947 and after) constitute a major part of the literature of the Qumran monastery. The name is probably from the root of a Hebrew word meaning "pious." The Essenes endeavored to reach absolute religious purity through strict abstemiousness and cleanliness. Their common meals were regarded as sacrificial feasts. Their lives were divided between religious exercises, lustrations (purification ceremonies), and labor at tillage and handicrafts. They had a community of goods and disapproved of marriage. They forbade trading, swearing of oaths, and anointing with oil. They sent gifts of incense to the Temple at Jerusalem, but differed from orthodox Judaism in their rejection of all animal sacrifices, in praying daily at sunrise, and in their view of the body as essentially evil and incapable of resurrection. The principles in which they differed from Judaism may have been derived from the East. They are not mentioned in the NT, and by the time of our Lord appear to have had little or no influence on the life of their nation.

Es'ther

A Jewess of Susa who became the queen of Ahasuerus, and frustrated a plot to destroy all Jews. This is commemorated in the Jewish festival of Purim.

Es'ther, the Book of

The last of the OT historical books, it contains an early example of pre-Christian anti-Semitism. Esther, a Jewess, was chosen as the new queen for Ahasuerus, the king of Persia. Her uncle Mordecai had incurred the enmity of Haman, the evil court favorite, and so brought the threat of death to his people. Esther, through her position, was able to avert the tragedy and save her people.

Eth'a·nim

The 7th month in the Hebrew calendar, later called Tishri.

E·thi·o'pi·a

An ancient name of the territory S of Egypt, also called Cush, and including what was subsequently called Sudan. From about 2000 B.C. there was sporadic warfare with Egypt. For some hundreds of years the area was independent of Egypt as the Kingdom of Nubia, with Napata as its capital. Later it was subdued in the expansion of the Assyrian empire.

Eu·phra'tes

The largest river in W Asia, called "the river" and "the great river." It flows from the mountains of Armenia to the Persian Gulf, 1700 mi.; 140 mi. above the Gulf, it is joined by the Tigris. The region between the rivers is thence called Mesopotamia.

ex'ile

Israel's geographical position made the country a buffer between Egypt to the W and the Assyrians and Babylonians to the E, involved in their almost constant warfare. In 721 B.C. the Assyrian Sargon II captured Samaria, the capital of the Northern Kingdom, and recorded in his inscriptions that he deported 27,290 Israelites to the E. With this deportation the identity of the N ten tribes disappeared; they were assimilated into the Assyrian population. People from the E were moved into Palestine. A century and a half later, after Babylonia had defeated Assyria, Jerusalem was captured; in 578 B.C. King Jehoiachin and some 10,000 of the population were deported to Babylon. An abortive rebellion led to further deportations in 587 B.C., and a reprisal deportation as a penalty for the assassination of the Babylon-appointed governor of Judah occurred in 582 B.C. Many of those deported were absorbed into the population of Babylonia, but following 538 B.C., the return from exile began, and with it the rebuilding of the temple.

Ex′o·dus

The return of the Hebrew people from Egypt to Israel is called the exodus from Egypt. The easy route had Egyptian fortifications scattered along the way, hence was avoided. It was for them, as a consequence, a journey of immense difficulty through wilderness and wild terrain, related in the Book of Exodus.

Ex′o·dus, the Book of

The second book of the OT relates the history of the Israelites from after the death of Joseph to the erection of the Tabernacle by Moses. It includes an account of the wanderings in the wilderness of Sinai and the giving of the law to the nation.

ex′or·cists

Persons who professed to expel evil spirits by adjuration or the performance of certain rites. Strolling exorcists were very numerous in the first century, especially in Asia Minor. Some of them undertook, instead of their usual formulas, to employ the name of Jesus (Acts 19.13).

E·ze′ki·el

(Heb. "God strengthens") A Jewish prophet, son of a priest Buzi, was among the captives whom Nebuchadnezzar carried with king Jehoiachin in 598 B.C. to Babylonia, where he settled near the river Chebar. His prophetic work extended over not less than 22 years (592-570).

E·ze′ki·el, the Book of

This OT book is written by the prophet of the exile. It is divided into two sections; the first denounces the sins and abominations of Jerusalem and the second looks to the future with the hope that the city will be restored after it has been cleansed. This latter section contains passages strongly messianic in nature.

Ez′ra, Ez′rah

(Heb. "Yahweh helps") The name of 3 persons in the OT, one of whom, a priest and scribe, was the organizer of the post-Exilic community. With the favor and support of Artaxerxes Longimanus, he led a band of 1800 male Israelites from Persia to Palestine in 458 B.C. to strengthen Zerubbabel's colony. He carried out a drastic reform by casting out the foreign wives and their children, and established a regular synagogue service, in which the chief place was given to reading and exposition of the Law. For this service he founded the special class of Scribes. Ezra exercised a most powerful influence on the development of Judaism. The complete subjection of the people under the Law was the fruit of his work (Ezra 7–10; Neh 8–10, and 12).

Ez'ra, the Book of

Ezra and Nehemiah are companion OT books, continuing the narration of Chronicles. Ezra details the first return of the Jews from their captivity in Babylon and the rebuilding of the Temple.

F

fal'low deer, roe'buck

More than one variety of deer can be found in the Near and Middle East, but the precise species to which reference is made has not been identified (Deut 4.5; 1 Kings 4.23).

fast'ing

Complete or partial abstinence from food is an expression of religious humiliation in the OT, often described by the phrase, "to afflict the soul." It was regarded as the natural sign of sorrow, especially of penitence; and where this mood, which gives fasting its value, is wanting, the prophets condemn it as displeasing to God (Jer 14.12). The only regularly recurring fast prescribed by the law is "from even till even" on the great Day of Atonement. After the Exile the days of national calamity were commemorated with fasting: the 10th day of the 10th month (Tebeth), the day of the beginning of the siege by Nebuchadnezzar; the 9th day of the 4th month (Tammuz), when the city was taken: the 7th day of the 5th month (Ab), when the Temple was destroyed, and in the 7th month (Tishri), the day of Gedaliah's murder. Fasting came to be regarded as meritorious in itself. The Pharisees fasted twice a week; on the 5th day of the week, when Moses was believed to have gone up to Mount Sinai and on the 2nd, when he was supposed to have descended. John's disciples fasted often. Our Lord imposed no fasting on His disciples while He was with them, but did not condemn the practice when followed in a right spirit, and He fasted before the beginning of His ministry. The first Christians fasted, in particular before the mission of Apostles and the appointment of elders. Paul's fastings appear to have been involuntary. The RSV excludes, on the evidence of the MSS, the references to fasting in Mt 17.21; Mk 9.29; Acts 10.30; 1 Cor 7.5.

fa'ther

The title of the First Person in the Godhead. God was revealed and known as the Father of His chosen people under the Old Testament dispensation and in a fatherly relation to individuals; but it was peculiarly the function of Christ to reveal the Fatherhood of God, and to bring men back to this relationship, as it is the function of the Spirit to seal and testify to this relationship of God and the believer.

feasts

The 3 annual festivals of the sanctuary were: (1) the Passover, (2) The Feast of Weeks, (3) the Feast of Tabernacles.

1. *The Passover* commemorated the deliverance of the Israelites from Egypt. It began on the 14th of Abib or Nisan in the evening, i.e. in the beginning of the 15th day, with a sacrificial meal, when a lamb or kid was roasted whole, and was eaten with bitter herbs and unleavened bread by the members of every family, and the head of the household recited the history of the redemption from Egypt. The sacrifices denoted expiation and dedication; the bitter herbs recalled the bitterness of the Egyptian bondage; unleavened bread was an emblem of purity.

2. *The Feast of Weeks* or of Harvest, or Day of Firstfruits or Pentecost (Gr. "fiftieth"), held on the 50th day or 7 weeks after the second day of the Passover, was the 2nd of the 3 annual festivals of the Sanctuary. It was limited to a single day, for only a portion of the products of the year had been garnered. Two loaves of leavened bread, representing the firstfruits of the grain harvest, were offered to the Lord. Ten suitable animals were sacrificed as a burnt offering, a kid for a sin offering, and 2 lambs for a peace offering.

3. *The Feast of Tabernacles,* or Ingathering,

was the last of the 3 annual festivals. It was appointed to take place in the 7th month, at the close of the agricultural season, when all the products of the year had been gathered. It was celebrated during 7 days: The daily burnt offering included a total of 70 bullocks, distributed by a decreasing scale over the 7 days, and in addition 2 rams and 14 lambs daily, and as a sin offering a he-goat was daily sacrificed. During its celebration the people dwelt in booths made of the boughs of trees.

fer'ret, geck'o

A lizard such as the gecko is probably intended. A ferret is related to the weasel.

fig

This fruit is frequently mentioned in Scriptures, and indigenous to Palestine. These figs appear in February before the leaves, which do not cover the tree until a month or six weeks later. When the leaves are fully out, the fruits should be ripe.

fir

See Pine.

fish'es

The fishes of Palestine include several different species. The fishes of the Jordan and Lake Tiberias are extremely like those of the Nile. They are carplike, large-scaled fishes, barbels, dace and bleak, loaches, etc. The Phoenicians engaged in sea-fishing.

fitch'es

An archaic spelling for vetch, a legume. It

probably should be translated as the word *spelt* rather than as any variety of vetch.

flax

This fiber was grown in Egypt and Palestine from very early times. The tabernacle hangings and the high priest's dress were of linen (Ex 27–29).

flea

This insect is only twice mentioned in the Bible, where David compares himself to a flea, a thing too insignificant for Saul to pursue. Fleas are, however, a real pest in the Holy Land, as in most other Mediterranean countries, the huts and camps of the natives swarming with them (1 Sam 24.16; 26.20).

flood

There are among native tribes of the Americas, the Pacific Islands and Australia and the early peoples of Mesopotamia, many stories of floods resembling that of the time of Noah. As re-

Coin of Apamea depicting Noah and ark.

lated in Gen 6–9, God found the mankind He
had created to be wicked, and decided upon its
destruction. Noah was a righteous man and was
to be spared, he was instructed to build an
ark, and to take into it 2 of every species of
animal, with provisions, and with his wife, their
3 sons, and the sons' wives. God closed the ark
and the rains came, flooding the entire earth.
Some time after the rains stopped, Noah sent
forth successively a raven and a dove to learn
whether or not the waters had gone down.
When on its 3rd flight the dove did not return,
Noah knew that the bird had found a resting

Flood tablet from Nippur, Babylonia, bearing one of
the earliest stories of the flood, and the fall of man.
The language is Sumerian.

place, and the ark was again opened. The biblical statement is that the ark rested on Ararat. Archaeologists have been refused permission to search for it, as Ararat overlooks Soviet territory.

fly

Two Hebrew words are taken to mean fly, one the ordinary housefly, the other the large horsefly. The stinging fly, the 4th of the plagues visited on the Egyptians, is a separate word in the Hebrew.

food, laws regarding

In the law all animals are divided into the clean, which might be eaten, and the unclean, which are forbidden. It distinguishes as clean the beasts which both chew the cud and have parted hooves; fishes with fins and scales; all birds except 19 or 20, mostly carnivorous; and among creeping things, the locust. Laws more or less similar are found among the Egyptians, Hindus, Persians, and Muslims. The distinction between clean and unclean food before it was established in God's name in the law was a settled custom and tradition among the Jews, perhaps originally derived from the natural repugnance and loathing at the sight, or touch, or smell of many animals, from ill effects on health traced to various meats, and from the place which, e.g., swine's flesh, had in the customs of heathen idolatry. The purpose for which this traditional distinction of clean from unclean meats was elevated into a formal law is distinctly expressed; it was to form a part of the partition wall that should separate from the Gentiles the people chosen by Jehovah for His own possession. All those parts of animals which, according to the sacrificial ritual, were consecrated to the altar, were forbidden under severe penalties; especially blood, for (1) "the life of all flesh is the blood thereof," and must be given back to the Lord of life; and (2) blood was set apart to make atonement for the soul. Contrast the practice of the heathen, e.g., the Philistines, who in their idolatry drank the blood reeking in the sacrificial basin. Certain pieces of the fat of such animals as were suitable for sacrifices (oxen, sheep, and goats) were not to be eaten, but were consecrated to the Lord. It was forbidden also "to seethe a kid in his mother's milk," which might possibly be taken as equivalent to eating flesh with the blood, and thus forbidden to the Hebrews along with the blood sacraments of the heathen; present-day Arabs sometimes stew a lamb or kid in milk. The flesh of animals that had been strangled or killed without being bled in the regular manner and flesh that had been sacrificed to heathen idols were likewise forbidden. Except in times of great distress or of religious decline these laws were well observed. The scrupulousness of the Jews in regard to these laws of food rendered it difficult for Jewish Christians and Gentile Christians to eat together and enjoy full religious fellowship; a compromise was therefore agreed to by the Gentile Christians to meet the Jewish Christians on this point. Christ declared

the whole of this legislation to be morally indifferent.

fox

In Ps 63.10 and Lam 5.18 the translation should
be jackal rather than fox.

frank′in·cense

A fragrant gum resin imported into Palestine
from Arabia.

freed′men

See Libertines.

frog

Frogs are mentioned in the OT only in connec-
tion with the second Egyptian plague.

front′lets and arm′lets

The same as phylacteries (Ex 13.16; Deut 6.8).
To carry out the injunction of the Law literally,
four passages (Ex 13.1-10, 11-16; Deut 6.4-9;
11.13-21) were copied on strips of parchment,
enclosed in a leather case, and bound by a
strap around the head or around the left arm.

G

G

Ga·la′tia

A Roman province in central Asia Minor. Its
S portion was in Paul's missionary field.

Ga·la′tians

The Letter of Paul to the Galatians, written in
A.D. 57 or 58, probably from Antioch, is the
cornerstone of Christian freedom. In Galatians
Paul tells of his own conversion and of how he
stood firm in his belief that Christ was the

Savior of people everywhere, not just those who observed every detail of the Jewish law.

gal'ba·num

A resinous juice used for the sacred incense.

Gal·i·le'ans

The people of Galilee being little under the influence of Jerusalem, the center of Jewish piety and culture, were looked down upon as ignorant rustics. They bitterly resented, however, the Roman yoke and supplied a large proportion of the Zealots.

Gal'i·lee

The region between Samaria on the W, the river Leontes on the S, the maritime plain on the N, and the Sea of Galilee, including its E coast, on the E. Exclusive of the lake, it measured about 50 mi. N and S, by 25 to 35 E and W. It included the plain of Esdraelon; Lower Galilee, a series of parallel ranges, none over 1,850 ft.; and Upper Galilee in the N, a series of plateaus surrounded by hills from 2,000 to 4,000 ft. high. The line between the two Galilees ran from the N end of the lake, W to Acre. Galilee is well watered and wooded, with stretches of good grain land. Earthquakes are frequent. The greatest thoroughfare is the so-called Way of the Sea, connecting Damascus with the Levant.

Gal'i·lee, the Sea of

In a great ditch 680 ft. below the level of the sea is the Sea of Galilee, 13 mi. long by 8 broad. On the W lay Tiberias; Magdala and Taricheae, where the fish were cured, were probably to the S. On the NW are Capernaum and Chorazin. Bethsaida is on the E of Jordan. On the eastern shore lay Gergesa. Gadara was about 5 mi. from the SE corner of the lake, about 2300 ft. above it.

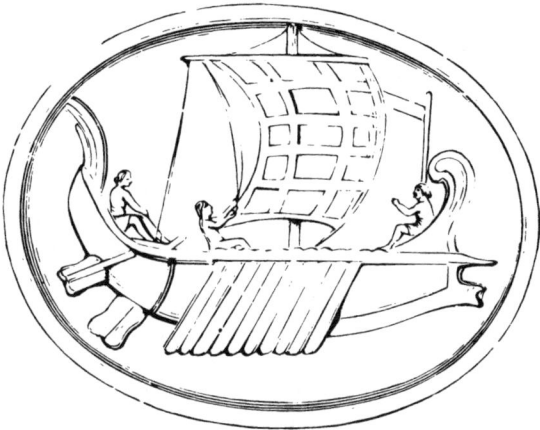

Roman galley

G

gall

A bitter, poisonous herb, possibly the same as the hemlock of Socrates.

gar'lic, gar'lick

A bulb of the lily family. Egyptian inscriptions list it, and during their wandering in the wilderness the Hebrews longed for it.

gate

In most Hebrew towns the only open space was just within the gate or gates. There the market was held, disputes were decided, and business of all kinds was transacted. The gate was the center of the social life of the place.

Ga'za

A famous Philistine city in SW Palestine, close to the sea. It retained its importance as a caravan depot in all ages. Little excavating has been done because of the modern city on the site of the old. *See also* Gezer.

geck'o

A lizard. *See* Ferret.

gems

Three lists of gems occur in the Bible: the high priest's breastplate (Ex 28); the ornaments of the king of Tyre (Ezek 28); the foundations of the heavenly Jerusalem (Rev 21).

Gems do not occur naturally in Palestine, and no great numbers have been found in excavations there, as compared with Egypt and Mesopotamia where many jewels have been found in tombs and temples. Faceted cutting was not understood, or at least not practiced, in the ancient world, but their engraving of jewels was fully as expert as anything done today.

Gen'e·sis

The first book of the OT that contains the account of God's creation of man and the universe. The book has two main divisions. The first is the history of early mankind, narrating the events of the Creation, the Fall, the Flood, and the Dispersion. The second section concerns the lives of Abraham, Isaac, Jacob, and Joseph.

Gen·nes′a·ret
A fertile plain on the shore of the Sea of Gali-lee. Also, an early name for the Sea of Galilee.

Ger′i·zim, Mount
Modern Jebel el-Tor, 2900 ft., directly S of Mount Ebal.

Geth·sem′a·ne
A garden at the foot of the Mount of Olives, where Judas betrayed Jesus. Its exact position is not known.

Ge′zer, Ga′zer, Ga·za′ra, Ga·ze′ra, Ga′za
Now called Tell el-Jazari, this site was excavated at the beginning of the 20th century. It had been a settlement at least since 4000 B.C.

G

Gid′e·on
(Heb. "hewer," "slasher") He tore down the Baal altar of his family and destroyed the Asherah. He was answered regarding his fitness to save Israel by having his fleece remain dry while the floor around it was wet with dew, and vice versa; he had other miraculous experiences. By a ruse he routed the Midianites. He was liberator and reformer but refused to be made king.

gier
See Eagle.

Gi′hon
An intermittent spring in the Kidron Valley beneath the City of David.

Gil·bo′a, Mount
Modern Jebel Fuqu'ah, at the E end of the Val-ley of Jezreel 6 mi. W of Beth-shean; eleva-tion 1737 ft.

Gil'e·ad

(Heb. "monument of stones") 1. The name of 2 persons and a family in the OT.

2. A region E of the Jordan between the Yarmuk and Arnon rivers. It is a well-watered and fertile region, suitable for grapes and olives. Well forested, it is the source of balm of Gilead, an aromatic resin regarded as having medicinal properties and exported to Egypt and Phoenicia.

Gil'e·ad, Mount

There is no single Mount Gilead; the entire area is rugged, above the Jordan Valley, at this point 700 ft. below sea level.

Gil'gal

(Heb. "circle of stones") The name of several places in the OT. One lies E of Jericho, in the Jordan Valley. Possibly it is the modern Khirbet Mefjir. Another is probably the modern Jil-julieh, on the top of a high hill 7 mi. N of Bethel. This is the Gilgal of Elijah and Elisha. Another Gilgal has been compared with Haro-sheth-ha-Goiim but has not been definitely identified. It has been placed in Samaria, in Sharon, and elsewhere. One Gilgal near She-chem has been suggested and another is said to be on the road from Jericho to Jerusalem.

gnats, lice

Being among the smallest of insects they are used in metaphors to emphasize contrast, for example, to a bulky animal such as the camel.

goats

An important item in the pastoral wealth of the Near East since biblical times. They are reared alongside of but not with the sheep. The sheep close graze the tender herbage; the goats browse on the twigs of the bushes. Goats' milk is preferred to any other.

goat, wild

The Sinaitic ibex. The Hebrew is translated always by "wild goat," except in Prov 5.19, where the feminine form is rendered "roe." Another word, akko, occurs only in Deut 14.5, where it is translated "wild goat." The Sinaitic ibex is a very beautiful creature, of a light fawn color, with very long recurved and regularly knotted horns, smaller and more slender than the Alpine and Himalayan species.

G

Gog and Ma'gog

Gog, prince of Meshech, who came from a land called Magog, is in Ezek 38–39 the leader of the forces of evil in a battle with Yahweh. In Rev 20.8 Magog is a leader with Gog of the forces of Satan in the battle of Armageddon.

gold

This metal apparently was not obtained in Palestine; some was imported from Sheba (part of Arabia), some from Ophir. The last district has been identified both with the W coast of India and with some part of the E coast of Africa. Some came from Nubia by way of Egypt. Gold, as we know from the contents of ancient graves, was in use for ornamental purposes at a very early date, even when stone held the place of metal for weapons and tools. It was no doubt obtained (and this is still a source of supply) by washing the river sands and other alluvial deposits.

Gol'go·tha

(Heb. "skull") The place of the crucifixion of Jesus.

Go·mor'rah

One of the 5 cities of the Valley mentioned with Sodom, Admah, Zeboim, and Zoar. Believed to be under the water of the S end of the Dead Sea.

go'pher wood

Not definitely identified.

Go'shen

The name of 3 places in the OT. One is presumably the area between Hebron and the Negev. Another is sometimes identified with modern Zahariyeh, 12 mi. SW of Hebron. The 3rd is the area of Egypt where the Israelites were from the time of Joseph until the Exodus.

gourd

The bottle gourd is used for booths and trellises in the Near East, and may be the plant mentioned in Jonah 4. The castor bean has also been suggested. The wild gourd has a poisonous fruit. At Gilgal during a famine, men were poisoned by it and appealed to Elisha for help. The vine of Sodom was probably the wild gourd.

grass' hop·per, lo'cust

"Locust" is sometimes used for the gregarious phase of certain short-horned grasshoppers. The grasshopper destroys vegetation at all stages of its life.

Grasshopper

Gre'cians
Greek-speaking Hebrews.

grey' hound
The greyhound is shown in Assyrian sculptures; the meaning of the Hebrew of Prov 30.31 is uncertain, but this dog may have been known in Palestine.

grind'ing
Grain was ground into flour in handmills or querns consisting of two hard circular stones, one revolved upon the other by means of a peg or handle. The labor was commonly performed by women. The Law forbade any one to take another's millstone in pledge.

grove
See Asherah.

H

Ha·bak'kuk
A prophet of Judah in the last days of Josiah (640-609 B.C.) and the reign of Jehoiakim (609-598 B.C.).

Ha·bak′kuk, the Book of
An OT book of prophecy concerned with the problem of unpunished evil in the world. It was revealed to Habakkuk that the Chaldean armies were to be God's means of punishing the wicked and that evil would destroy itself. The book concludes with a poem of thanksgiving and great faith.

Hag·ga′da, Hag·ga′dah
(Heb. "narration") The name for that part of the traditions of the Jewish scribes consisting of the elaboration of the historical and didactic portions of Scripture. As contrasted with the Halacha, which confined itself to the exposition and application of the text, its handling of the Scripture is unrestrained. It freely admits additions and interpolations, including legends.

Hag′ga·i
A Jewish prophet who came forward at Jerusalem, in 529 B.C., to urge the rebuilding of the Temple.

Hag′ga·i, the Book of
This OT book is a report on the utterances of the prophet Haggai during the second year of the reign of Darius, king of the Persian Empire, in the post-exilic period. The prophet is singularly concerned with the rebuilding of the Temple, which was essential to restoring the nation's religious purity. Haggai also believed that a great messianic age was at hand.

Hag·i·og′ra·pha
(Heb. "writings") The third division of the books included in the Hebrew Canon have a

more diversified character than either Law or Prophecy, and they have never received a more definite designation.

hair

The Hebrews regarded a strong growth of hair both on the head and on the chin as an ornament to a man. By many it was worn hanging down to the shoulder. To cut off a man's beard was to offer him the grossest insult. Only in times of mourning was the head shaved. That the hair was also worn in locks or ringlets is shown by the case of Samson.

Ha·la·cha′

(Heb. "that which is current") The Rabbinical law of custom, which was developed beside the written Torah or Law of Moses. It was distinguished from the Haggada as being the legal part of the oral tradition of the scribes, including their expositions of the Torah, and all the additional laws which were recognized as binding by the Jews after the Exile.

Hal·lel′, Hal·le·lu′jah

(Heb. "praise ye the Lord") Probably sung in unison by the Temple choir.

Ham

1. The name of Noah's second son.

2. A city E of the Jordan, attacked by Chedorlaomer. Tell Ham, the ruin of the ancient city, is near modern Ham on the Wadi er-Rejeilah.

3. A poetic synonym for Egypt, used several times in the Psalms.

Ha'math

A town on the Orontes in Syria, the modern Nahr el-Asi. Excavation revealed 12 layers, going back to Neolithic times. It is one of the important centers of Hittite inscriptions. It made alliance with David, and in 740 B.C. with Azariah (against Assyria). Conquered by the Assyrians in 720 B.C., the people of Hamath were transported to Samaria.

hang'ings

See Cotton.

Ha'ran

Now Harran, in Turkey, a city devoted to the moon cult, where Abraham stopped on his journey from Ur to Canaan.

hare

Though the name occurs only in the lists of Leviticus and Deuteronomy, there is no question about the translation, the hare being very common, and the Arabic name the same as the Hebrew. It was forbidden as food to the Israelites because it does not divide the hoof, even though (Moses parenthetically adds) it chews the cud, i.e., re-chews.

harp

A 10-string harp has been found in an Egyptian tomb of 1000 B.C., an earlier wooden one of 1550 B.C., and a golden lyre at Ur. The harp, lute and cithern are similar; David's harp, however, seems to have been more properly a lyre.

hart, hind

Fallow deer, habitat Syria, now almost if not altogether extinct in Palestine, must have been very common in ancient times. Deer are often depicted on the monuments both of Egypt and Assyria. The bones of the red deer have been found in caverns in Lebanon.

Har'vest, Feast of
One of the 3 great annual festivals, held at the end of the agricultural year. Also called the *Feast of Ingathering. See* Feasts.

hawk
The bird mentioned is not positively identified.

head-dress
The common head-dress of the people was probably like that of the modern Bedouin—a colored handkerchief bound round the head with a cord so as to shade both neck and ears from the sun. In later times the rich wore a turban formed of a long strip of fine linen rolled many times round the head. Yet another "headtire" was worn on festive occasions, especially by brides or bridegrooms.

heath
See Juniper.

He'brews
The descendants of Eber (Gen 10.21). They may have been a separate ethnic group, but were closely related to the Israelites; the names in some circumstances became interchangeable.

He'brews, the Let'ter to the
An anonymous NT book which urges the Hebrew Christian community not to fall back into Judaism and argues for Christian superiority.

He'bron
An ancient city in the high mountains of Judah,

19 mi. S of Jerusalem. The modern town, el-Khalil, surrounds the cave of Machpelah.

hedge'hog

The Hebrew word has also been translated "bittern" and "porcupine." Porcupines are found in modern Palestine.

Hel'len·ists

Greek-speaking Jews, in Judea or abroad, many of whom had adopted a measure of Greek (Hellenic) culture and manners.

hem'lock

A poisonous plant or one with a bitter root, also translated gall or wormwood. The plant most probably meant grows in waste places in Palestine, a perennial 3 to 4 ft. tall, with leaves resembling a carrot's.

hen'na, cam'phire

A fragrant flowering shrub. A dye prepared from the crushed leaves mixed with water is used to color the soles of the feet, palms, and nails.

Her'mon, Mount

The S spur of the anti-Lebanon, elevation 9100 ft., and frequently snow-covered. It is visible from many places in Palestine.

Her'od the Great

The founder of the dynasty that ruled Palestine 37 B.C.-A.D. 70, was the son of Antipater, an Idumaean, who had been Asmonaean governor in Edom, and who rose to a position of great influence as the minister of Hyrcanus II, the last Asmonaean king and high-priest. Antipater saw that the future of Judaea was in the hands of Rome and cunningly ingratiated himself first with Pompey, then, after his death, with Julius Caesar (who rewarded his assistance with men and money in Egypt in 48 B.C. by making him governor of Judaea, Samaria, and Galilee, under the nominal sovereignty of Hyrcanus), and after Caesar's assassination in 44 B.C., with Cassius, Antonius and Augustus. Herod consistently followed his father's policy and took advantage of all the vicissitudes of Roman affairs. He saw himself at last the "confederate king" (*rex socius*) of the Roman emperor. A decree of the Roman senate made him king of Judaea in 40 B.C. In 37 B.C. he married Mariamne, granddaughter of Hyrcanus, and with the help of two Roman legions, captured Jerusalem. The next 9 years he spent in strengthening his position. He executed 45 members (the Sadducee majority) of the Sanhedrin and murdered every member of the Asmonaean house, including his wife Mariamne. The next 14 years (28-14 B.C.) were chiefly devoted to the erection of public buildings, including a theater in Jerusalem and a great amphitheater outside the gates, as well as numerous heathen temples and new cities, the chief of which was Caesarea, named after the emperor. His greatest work was the rebuilding of the Temple. But the golden eagle, the symbol of Roman supremacy, which he placed over its chief entrance, was to the people a continual reminder of his subservience to Rome. All the material advantages of his despotic rule, the tranquility of the country, his remissions of taxation and encouragement of trade and agriculture, his provision for the poor in time of scarcity, were forgotten. His life was constantly threatened by conspiracies, which he fought with secret police and the most cruel torture. In the year 7 B.C. he caused Alexander and Aristobulus, his 2 sons by Mariamne, to be strangled at Samaria, a crime which led Augustus to remark that he would rather be one of Herod's swine than one of his sons. Another son, Antipater, who had tried to assassinate his father, was executed 5 days before the death of Herod in 4 B.C. His sons shared his dominions according to his will. The elder, Archelaus, ethnarch of Judaea, Samaria, and Idumaea, was deposed by Augustus for misgovernment in A.D. 6, and died in Gaul. The eastern and northern provinces fell to Philip, who died in A.D. 34. Herod Antipas, who received Galilee and Peraea, was deposed by Caligula in A.D. 39. The Herod of Acts 12 was a grandson of Herod "the Great," and was surnamed Agrippa. He obtained from Caligula the inheritance of Philip, and also that of Antipas, to which Claudius added Judaea and Samaria, so that from A.D. 41 to 44, he ruled over the whole of Palestine. He succeeded by cunning and hypocrisy in gaining the confidence of the people. His son, Herod Agrippa II (Acts 25, 26), after doing all in his power to dissuade the Jews from making war against the Romans, took their side against his countrymen, and after Jerusalem was taken, lived chiefly at Tiberias as a Roman vassal prince till he died childless in A.D. 100.

He·ro'di·ans

A political and nonpatriotic minority, in the main a court party, which stood to the Idumaean dynasty of the Herods in Galilee much as the Sadduceean nobility stood to the Roman procurator in Judaea. They made less pretense, however, of aiming higher than at worldly prosperity. Their natural enemies were the strict Pharisees; and it is a mark of the shifts to which both parties were driven in their hatred of Jesus that they united to work His ruin. The "leaven of Herod" (Mk 8.15) was worldly wisdom.

Hez·e·ki'ah

(Heb. "Yah is my strength") The name of 4 persons in the OT, one of whom was King of Judah 715–687 B.C.

H

Hid'de·kel

The Hebrew name of the Tigris River.

high place, sanc'tu·ar·y

The Canaanites were worshiping their gods on high places when Abraham appeared in their country. Usually there were groves of trees associated with these hilltops and other sites. The sanctuary was a temple with an altar or an altar alone, with the altar often elevated. The Israelites were instructed by God to destroy the Canaanite high places and the groves and the altars, usually dedicated to a local god, but in this they were frequently remiss. At times the high places were simply taken over. Hezekiah was diligent in their destruction, but many of the kings were indifferent. The sanctuary won recognition only after a long period.

high priest

The chief in the priestly hierarchy. At times in Israel's history, the chief priest shared full honors with the king.

hind

See Hart.

Hin'nom

A deep valley S of Jerusalem, called variously the Valley of the Sons of Hinnom, Valley of the Children of Hinnom, Valley of Ben-Hinnom, and usually identified with the modern Wadi er-Rababi.

Hit'tites

First mentioned by Sargon of Agade about the end of the 3rd millennium, the Hittites came from N of the Taurus Mountains, and at an early date conquered part of N Syria. They made Carchemish on the Euphrates one of their capitals, and established themselves in Kadesh near Emesa. After years of war, Ramses II of Egypt made a treaty of peace with the Hittite king, probably between 1290 and 1280 B.C. Hittites had previously settled in the south of Palestine, at Hebron, and at Jerusalem. They had a number of small kingdoms, and seem to have extended over the greater part of Asia Minor as well as over N Syria. The westward conquest by the Assyrians overcame the Hittite kingdoms and their independent history ended with the capture of Carchemish by Sargon in 717 B.C. The Hittites used a peculiar hieroglyphic writing, not deciphered until after 1925. The Egyptian monuments agree with their own in representing them as short, thick-limbed, with protrusive jaw and nose, beardless face, high cheekbones, yellow skin, and black hair and eyes. Their language was of the Indo-European group.

Hi'vites

A nation in Canaan before the Israelites.

holm tree, cy'press

Sometimes identified with the evergreen holm oak; since the root of the word means "to be lean," sometimes translated "cypress."

Ho·ly Ghost', Ho·ly Spir'it

The third person of the Trinity, through whom the entire Godhead works with man.

Hor, Mount

This may be a mountain on the border of Edom, or a mountain near Petra, now called Jebel Harun, elevation 4800 ft.

hor'net

(Heb. "depression") Hornets belong to the same order of insects as bees and wasps and are closely allied to the latter. All these insects have four wings; they wound by a stinger lodged in the end of the abdomen, and inject a poisonous fluid into the wound.

horse

The horse was introduced in the Near East about the middle of the 2nd millennium B.C. Solomon brought the horse to Israel. The principal use was in warfare; the Israelites looked upon horses as a pagan luxury and a symbol of dependence on physical power rather than upon God. Nevertheless the use of the horse did increase, not only for war chariots but for transport. Israel's horses came from Egypt.

horse'leech

The horseleech (*haemopis sanguisuga*) and the medicinal leech (*hirudo medicinalis*) are both common in Palestine, as are several other kinds of leeches. The leeches abound in waters and damp places of hot countries and frequently become a regular pest, attacking men and animals alike.

Ho·se'a

(Heb. "salvation") The last of the great prophets of the Northern Kingdom.

Ho·se'a, the Book of

The first book of the twelve minor prophets in the OT. Because the times were outwardly prosperous, idolatry prevailed and immorality was rampant. Hosea urges a return to God in order that He may show mercy and forgiveness.

Ho·she'a

(Heb. "may Yah save") The name of 4 persons in the OT, one of whom was the last king of Israel.

house

(Heb. beth, common in compound names of places, as Beth-el) The nomad's house was his tent. The settled Hebrew dwelt generally in a one-story building with few and small windows, built of mud bricks or sun-dried brick, and flat-roofed. Here both the family and the animals found shelter, a raised dais separating the two.

But, except in bad weather, the family spent their day either in the open field or on the roof, where they also slept.

Hur'ri·ans

The name of an ancient people referred to variously as Horites, Hivites, Jebusites.

hy·e'na

The Hebrew word has also been translated "wild beast" and "speckled bird." The hyena has been the commonest of the carnivores of Palestine.

Hyk'sos kings

The Egyptian word for "rulers of foreign countries" was applied to the 15th and 16th dynasties in the Egyptian Delta. These foreigners, sometimes called the Shepherd Kings, had entered from the NE. The last ruler of the 17th dynasty at Thebes drove the Hyksos northward, and the first of the 18th dynasty expelled them from Egypt entirely in about 1550 B.C.

hys'sop

A bushy small plant, probably orégano or Syrian marjoram. The entire plant was used as a brush to sprinkle sacrificial blood. This use of the plant seems to have followed upon its use to mark the lintels of Hebrew homes at the 1st Passover.

I

i'bex

See Pygarg.

i'bis

The ibis is found in Egypt, but not in Palestine; it may have been native to Palestine in biblical times. The translation may be erroneous; the word has also been translated "great owl."

Im·man'u·el

(Heb. "God is with us") The name of the child whose birth was prophesied by Isaiah; in the NT it becomes a prophecy of the birth of Jesus.

In'gath·er·ing, Feast of

The Feast of Harvest. *See under* Feasts.

i'ron

It is probable that smelting iron ore and working iron began with the Hittites in the middle of the 2nd millennium B.C. The Philistines may have brought it to Palestine, but they permitted no Hebrew smiths. All iron work had to be taken to the Philistines. But gradually a supply of iron was imported, and iron slag is found in the Arabah, indicating that there was some native iron industry.

I'saac

(Heb. "he laughs") The son of Abraham and Sarah and half-brother of Ishmael was born when his parents were advanced in age. By his wife Rebekah he was the father of Jacob and Esau. He died at Hebron at the age of 180.

I·sa'iah

(Heb. "Yahweh is salvation") The son of Amoz, he prophesied in the reigns of Uzziah, Jotham, Ahaz, and Hezekiah, kings of Judah. Tradition says that he survived into the reign of Manasseh and was martyred by him. He advocated the policy of the separateness of Israel, opposing the Assyrian alliance of Ahaz and equally opposing all alliances with the neighboring peoples, with Egypt, or with the Babylonian-Elamitic combination against Assyria. During his life, the Assyrian and Babylonian empires were part of the time identical, the great oppressing power; and part of the time Babylon was a dangerous seducer, striving to lead the chosen people into disastrous hostilities with Assyria.

I·sa'iah, the Book of

This OT book is the first collection of prophecy of the five major Hebrew prophets. Judgment to come is fundamental to Isaiah's teaching. Israel and Judah are to perish but a remnant will survive and a new Jerusalem will rise up as a city of the faithful. It is also in Isaiah that memorable prophecies of Christ's coming are found.

Ish'ma·el

(Heb. "may God hear") The name of 6 persons in the OT, one of whom is Abraham's son, by Hagar. He is Isaac's half brother.

Ish'ma·el·ite

The wandering people of N Arabia, descendants of Ishmael, who were found in that region from the early 2nd millennium B.C. to the 7th century B.C.

Ish'tar

The Babylonian fertility goddess, Ashtoreth, in Palestine.

Is'ra·el

(Heb. "he who striveth with God," or "God striveth") The new name that Jacob received after his mysterious struggle at the Jabbok and hence the name of the whole people descended from him. The name "Hebrews" was mostly applied to them by foreigners, as was also the name "Jews," which arose at the time when Judah, after the fall of the Northern Kingdom, represented the entire people. After the separation under Jeroboam, the name Israel was con-

JUDAH
76,500

DAN
64,400

ISSACHAR
64,300

ZEBULUN
60,500

ASHER
53,400

MANASSEH
52,700

BENJAMIN
45,600

NAPHTALI
45,400

LEVI
23,000

REUBEN
43,730

GAD
40,500

EPHRAIM
32,500

SIMEON
22,200

Relative size of the 12 tribes of Israel, based on the number of men of military age

fined to the kingdom of the ten tribes, also called Ephraim after the chief of these. Moral and religious degeneracy, with frequent revolutions and changes of rulers, prepared its fall (722 B.C.). The Assyrians led the best of the people into exile, from which they never returned, and the remnant left was included in the mixed people known as the Samaritans.

It'a·ly

The peninsula in the middle of Southern Europe. The name was applied at different periods to the whole peninsula and to the southern part.

Iy'yar

A name of the 2nd month of the Hebrew year. It is also called Ziv.

J

ja'cinth, lig'ure

A variety of zircon, a reddish-orange stone.

Ja'cob

(Heb. "he overreaches") The son of Isaac and Rebekah and father of the people of Israel, he gained by craft the birthright and blessing that his father meant for his brother Esau. He fled to his uncle Laban, who treated him with cunning equal to his own. Yet he enriched himself in Laban's service and Laban's daughters, Leah and Rachel, became his wives. On his return, after a mysterious struggle in the darkness of night at the Jabbok, his name was changed to Israel and he was reconciled to Esau. His old age was made sorrowful by evil deeds of his sons, till at last he found a refuge in Egypt with his favorite, Joseph.

James

The name of 5 persons in the NT.

1. "The elder," son of Zebedee and brother of John, one of the Twelve, was martyred under Herod Agrippa.

2. James "the younger," son of Alphaeus, was also an Apostle.

3. James "the brother of the Lord" was a pillar in the church at Jerusalem and had probably been led to believe by a special appearance of our Lord to him. His judgment prevailed in the council at Jerusalem. For his piety he was called James the Just. According to Josephus, he was stoned to death by order of Ananus the high priest, between the departure of Festus and the arrival of the new procurator Albinus.

4. A son of Mary.

5. The father of Judas.

James, the Let'ter of

This NT book, according to tradition written by the brother of our Lord, provides ethical instruction for all Jewish people who have become Christians. It is clear and practical in its dealing with Christian behavior.

Ja'pho

See Joppa.

jas'per

A green chalcedony.

Jeb'u·sites

The tribe that occupied Jerusalem at the time

of the Israelitish conquest of Canaan. They seem
to have been of the Amorite race.

Je·ho'a·haz

(Heb. "Yah has grasped") The name of 3 persons in the OT, one the King of Israel (815-
801 B.C.) and one King of Judah (609-608
B.C.).

Je·ho'ram

See Joram.

Je·hosh'a·phat

(Heb. "Yah judges") The name of 4 persons in
the OT, one of whom was King of Judah for
25 years, c. 850 B.C.

Je·ho'vah

The Hebrews did not commonly use the sacred
name, in the fear that it might be profaned. The
consonants of the name are four, called the
tetragrammaton. To these vowels may be added,
with the result that for a period of their history
the spoken name was Adoni, Lord, arrived at
by adding the vowels of that name to the consonants YHWH (JHVH). Misinterpretation of
this eventually led to Jehovah.

Je'hu

(Heb. "he is Yah") The name of 4 persons in
the OT, one of whom was King of Israel 842-
815 B.C.

Jeph'thah

(Heb. "he opens") A warrior of Gilead, a judge
in Israel and an illegitimate son, he was driven
from home by his father's heirs. He lived the
life of a freebooter in the land of Tob, east of
Jordan, until the elders of the tribes summoned

him to their help against the Amorites, who had oppressed them for 18 years. Returning a conquerer, he sacrificed his daughter, his only child, in fulfilment of a thoughtless vow.

Jer·e·mi'ah

(Heb. "may Yah lift up") The name of 10 persons in the OT, one of whom was Jeremiah the Prophet. Jeremiah's prophesying began in the 13th year of Josiah, 626 B.C., and covered the time following to the Exile. He was of priestly descent. His prophetic career began at an early age. In later years he was the leader of a small minority in Judah against 3 great wrongs: the religious apostasies of his people, their neglect of justice, and the false patriotism that led them to break faith by repeated revolts against Babylon. His services in this last matter were recognized by the Babylonian authorities.

Jer·e·mi'ah, the Book of

An OT account of the writing of certain of Jeremiah's prophecies, from dictation, by his friend Baruch. This seems to imply that these prophecies had been originally uttered without writing. As the roll of Baruch included "all" the prophecies for 23 years, besides "many like words," we are compelled to infer that most of the prophecies it contained were very briefly sketched. Jeremiah's mission was to testify to a doomed people, and then to witness their obduracy and their doom; but common opinion probably exaggerates the sorrowful element in the career of the "weeping prophet." It should be noticed that he prophesied concerning the return from the Exile, as well as concerning the Exile itself. It was especially his prophecies that actually led the exiles to the movement for return. Jeremiah insists especially upon the Lord's unfailing covenant with Israel and with David. He gives shape to the doctrine of a righteous "Branch" to grow up unto David. Like the other prophets, Jeremiah is a prophet not merely of rebuke and warning, but also of the Messianic promise and hope.

Jer'i·cho

An ancient city at the S end of the Jordan Valley, famous for its palms and gardens of balsam, which have now disappeared. It has been extensively excavated; carbon dating shows its oldest walls to date from 8000 to 7000 B.C.

Jer·o·bo'am

(Heb. "may the people grow numerous") The name of 2 kings of Israel, one of them Israel's 1st king, the son of Nebat, the founder of the N kingdom of Israel. He took advantage of the other tribes' envy of Judah and Jerusalem, and the general discontent with Solomon's oppressive taxation, to revolt against him. After the death of Solomon, on his son Rehoboam's blunt refusal to lighten the people's burdens, Jeroboam became the leader of the 10 northern tribes in their separation (922 B.C.). The reestablishment of the high places served to lend the political change a religious consecration. Golden calves and ox images, similar to those Aaron made in the wilderness, were set up at Dan in the north and Bethel on the southern frontier of Jeroboam's kingdom, to win the people away from the Temple at Jerusalem, where God was worshiped without images.

Jeroboam II ruled the kingdom of Israel from 786 to 746 B.C. He conquered in the N and E all the lands that had belonged to David and Solomon, and encouraged trade with the Phoenicians; but in his reign the Baal worship that Jehu had extirpated again arose, bringing with it the moral corruption in which Amos and Hosea foresaw the ruin of the king's house and of the nation.

Je·ru'sa·lem

(Heb. "foundation of Shalem") The chief city of Palestine, mentioned in Egyptian texts as early as the 19th and 18th centuries B.C., the 3rd most holy city of the Muslims and the most important to the Christians and Jews, the name of Jerusalem appears in more than 25 of the

Damascus Gate, the principal entry through the
north wall of Jerusalem

Sketch of a Roman medal commemorating the capture of Jerusalem.

books of the OT and in more than a dozen books of the NT.

Flints found in excavations in the area indicate very early inhabitants, and pottery from the 4th millennium B.C. has been found at Jerusalem itself. Abraham was once and quite possibly twice at Jerusalem, then called Salem or Shalem. The Jebusites were there before Abraham had entered Palestine; David captured the city and made it his capital, and Solomon built the Temple and made the city splendid.

In the almost incessant warfare of the last 2 millennia B.C., Jerusalem was often besieged and captured. It was at various times possessed by Assyria, Egypt, Babylonia, Persia, and Greece. Nebuchadnezzar sacked and destroyed the city, and took its people into exile. When they returned, they rebuilt the Temple and much of the city, but in A.D. 70 the Romans captured Jerusalem and devastated it so thoroughly that almost nothing of the time of Jesus remained. However, a city grew again on the ruins. The Crusaders held it for a time, as did the Turks. Israel recaptured Jerusalem on June 7, 1967.

Excavation has not been complete or thorough, because of the impossibility of carrying on such work in a densely populated area. Even so, a great number of the locations mentioned in the Bible have been identified and the life of Jerusalem in biblical times can be reconstructed.

Je·ru'sa·lem, the New

The principal city of God's new world that is to come, its spiritual capital, beautiful and adorned; an expression of the church of those who are of the people of God.

Jesh'u·a

See Joshua.

Je'sus

The coming of Jesus, the Christ, the Messiah, was anticipated in the OT; of His life on earth the Gospels are the source of what we know. Secular contemporary accounts are fragmentary. Calendars were not stabilized as today, and the precise date of His birth is not recorded. The earliest Church did not concern itself with the facts of His physical life on earth. He was Jesus, the man, and Christ, the Anointed One, a person of the Triune God. But by the 5th century the Church had concerned itself sufficiently to have set December 25 as the date of His birth. This had been the date of the festival of the sun god Mithra, and to the Christians a greater light was come, Jesus Christ, the true Light of the World.

Jesus was born in Bethlehem to Mary, the betrothed wife of Joseph, a carpenter. The genealogy is traced in the Gospels to David and to Abraham. The Gospels further· tell of the flight of the family to Egypt to avoid the slaughter of the Innocents by Herod the King, but say little of His early boyhood. The family lived the life of consecrated and pious Jews; Jesus must have had careful education and training, for at age 12 he talked on fully equal terms with the rabbis in the Temple.

Then follows another unrecorded period in His life. When a man of about 30 He was baptized by John the Baptist, who testified that this Jesus was the Son of God. After a great temptation to which He did not yield, He began His ministry, first calling His disciples. He was known by His works throughout Galilee and in adjacent areas, and attracted many followers, Jews and Greeks. But He disturbed many. He was arrested, tried, and crucified. There followed the Resurrection, the triumph over death. *See also* Christ.

Jew

The Bible provides definitions: 1. The members of the State of Judah (Neh 1.2; Jer 32.12; 40.11).

2. The post-exilic people of Israel in contrast to the Gentiles (Esther 9.15-19; Dan 3.8; Zech 8.23; John 4.9; Acts 14.1).

3. The adherents of worship of Yahweh as

done at Jerusalem after the Exile (Esther 3.4-6; Dan 3.8). In contrast to Gentiles, Samaritans, proselytes (John 2.6, 4.9, 22; Acts 2.10, 14.1). The term is now highly fluid. It covers religion and birth, religion only, or birth only.

Jewish history between the Testaments

The whole period falls into four epochs.

1. *Persian Period* (537-330 B.C.). Nehemiah (444 B.C.) had been a favorite at the court to which, 90 years before, the Jews had owed their return from Exile; and, on the whole, the restored remnant remained loyal to the "great king," in spite of the tribute and other galling features of their subjection. Many Jews, however, were removed to Babylonia and elsewhere by Artaxerxes Ochus, about 350 B.C., for taking part in a revolt. To the last century of Persian rule belong the final breach between the Jews and the Samaritans, the gradual replacement among the Jews of Hebrew by the widespread Aramaic dialect, and the beginning of the recovery of Galilee to the faith of Jehovah.

2. *Greek Period* (330-167 B.C.). Alexander the Great, who ushers in this period, besides granting special privileges to Jerusalem, bestowed marks of favor upon the Jews settled by him in his new city, Alexandria. It was here that Judaism entered into its most intimate relations with the Greek world of thought and literature. On Alexander's death (323 B.C.) his conque.. passed into the hands of his generals and, during the struggles that ensued, Palestine shared in the confusion, until the battle of Ipsus (301

B.C.) made the kings of Egypt (the Ptolemies) its overlords for a full century, in spite of several attempts on the part of the rival kings of Syria (the Seleucids) to overthrow them. The new sovereign power was both stronger and juster than the Persian; and under it the government at Jerusalem in the hands of the high-priestly dynasty, assisted by a sort of senate including the higher ranks of the priesthood, grew and consolidated. Outside Palestine, too, the Jews waxed influential, not only in Alexandria, but also in Libya, Cyrene, Asia Minor, and all parts of Syria, where they settled either by the compulsion or favor of Ptolemies and Seleucids. From the other side also foreign intercourse was fostered by Greek settlements in Northern Palestine, especially about the Sea of Galilee.

The most momentous outcome of all this was the Greek version of the Hebrew Scriptures, called the Septuagint, which did much to break down Jewish isolation, and fixed the type of language in which the NT is written. The influence of Hellenic culture was at work in both the life and the literature of the Jews during the Ptolemaic supremacy (320-198 B.C.), but its effects became clearer after 198 B.C., when Antiochus the Great brought Judea under Seleucid or Syrian sway.

The priestly nobility grew more worldly in spirit as Hellenism advanced. The high-priesthood became an object of base intrigue. Under Antiochus Epiphanes it became the fashion

among the upper classes to turn their names into
Greek forms, e.g., Menelaus for Menahem, and
in other ways to obscure their Jewish origin. At
length the folly of Antiochus and his high-
priestly tools led to a violent crisis and revolt.

3. *Maccabean or Asmonaean Period* (167-
63 B.C.). The outrages upon the national religion which stung the Maccabees into revolt
stirred the people to realize the value of their
distinctive faith. From their ranks had arisen
a party called the Chasidim, distinguished for
piety. The Maccabean movement carried these
with it, and became a rally of the whole nation
to the faith of its fathers. By the wars of libera-
tion from the yoke of Syria the religious end
was attained. The Temple was restored and
solemnly rededicated (165 B.C.), the rival temple on Mount Gerizim razed along with the
Samaritan capital itself (129 B.C.), and the
Maccabean leader recognized as "Governor and
High Priest for ever, until there should arise a
faithful prophet."

But the mass of the nation was now possessed by the spirit of foreign aggression; and
against this the successors of the quiet Chasidim, whose expectation was from God and not
from human agency, constantly protested. "The
idea of Judaism" was in danger in the eyes of
this growing party of religious protest, which in
the last years of Hyrcanus (135-106 B.C.) became known as Pharisees (Perushim, or "Separ-
atists"). These men, whose stronghold was
among the Scribes or professed students of the

Law, by degrees gained the ear of the people.
They indeed suffered a severe check under
Alexander Jannaeus (105-78 B.C.), in whose
favor a revulsion of popular feeling took place.
But the lost ground was more than made up
under his widow Salome (78-69 B.C.), who
separated the secular and sacred headship (her
son Hyrcanus II was high-priest). About this
time the Sanhedrin came more under the influence of the Scribes than heretofore; and so it
remained henceforth. On the death of Salome,
internal dissensions, centering round Hyrcanus
and his brother Aristobulus, gave the Romans
their chance. Under Pompey they occupied
Jerusalem, abolished the kingship, and restored
the high-priestly dignity to Hyrcanus.

4. *Roman Period*. While the Pharisees gained
by the change, which robbed the Sadducees of
political power, it sharpened the contrast between the Pharisaic ideal and the popular hope
of the restoration of the kingdom. It was especially galling when Antipater, of the hated
Idumaean race, became the real power in the
state under Rome till his death in 43 B.C., and
when in 37 B.C. his son Herod the Great became by Rome's aid king of Judea.

"By birth an Idumaean, by profession a Jew,
by necessity a Roman, by culture and by choice
a Greek," this unscrupulous monarch maintained himself only by inspiring fear. He filled
the chief offices with obscure men of priestly
descent from Babylon and Alexandria and abolished the life tenure of the high-priesthood. He

tried to overcome the national feeling against him by diverting attention to a great national object, the building of a new Temple, begun in 18 B.C. His death in 4 B.C. was the signal for an insurrection, which the Romans sternly repressed, handing over the country to 3 sons of Herod. Of these, Philip had the land east of Jordan; Antipas, Galilee and Perea; Archelaus, Judea and Samaria. After A.D. 6, Archelaus' kingdom passed under the direct rule of Rome, Pontius Pilate being procurator from A.D. 26 to 36.

Jo'ab

(Heb. "Yah is father") The name of 3 persons in the OT, one of whom was commander of David's army.

Jo'ash, Je·ho'ash

(Heb. "Yah gives") The name of 8 persons in the OT, one of whom was king of Judah (837-800 B.C.).

Job

1. The author of the Book of Job; unknown otherwise.

2. The name of the third son of Issachar, Iob, is sometimes written Job.

Job, the Book of

The first of the OT poetical books deals with the problem of suffering. God allows Satan to afflict Job, a prosperous and pious Jew, with many hardships in order to test his faith. Job loses his children and his worldly goods, and is afflicted by a terrible disease. Finally when God questions Job, he is forced to admit to the

limits of human wisdom, and bows humbly before the will of God. With this new humility his
faith is strengthened and Job finds peace.

Jo'el

(Heb. "Yah is God") The name of 13 persons
in the OT, one of whom is the author of the
Book of Joel. Nothing is known of him.

Jo'el, the Book of

This OT prophetical book was written during
a locust plague, a time of great distress for the
people. The prophet sees in the devastation of
the locusts an indication of the coming day of
the Lord. Therefore all must repent with fasting and mourning. With repentance, however,
there is a promise for relief and God's blessing
for Israel.

John

The name of 5 persons in the NT; one is John
the Baptist, another John the Apostle.

John the A·pos'tle

A son of Zebedee and brother of James, a fisherman, he has been called the Beloved Disciple.
At the time of the Crucifixion, Jesus committed
His mother to John's care. There is tradition
that he was banished to Patmos, and that he was
bishop at Ephesus for many years. He is considered the author of the Fourth Gospel, the
Letters of John, and the book of Revelation.

John the Bap'tist

The son of Elisabeth, who was related to Mary,
the Mother of Jesus, a prophet and descended
from priests. He has been called the forerunner
of Jesus, and was heeded by many for his own

message of the need for repentance. He was arrested by Herod and beheaded in prison.

John Mark

See Mark.

John, the Gos'pel according to

The Fourth Gospel, written by "the disciple whom Jesus loved," tells us who Jesus was and what He is; what He can always mean to those who love Him. This Gospel contains more than the other Gospels about the stories of Lazarus and Nicodemus and Jesus' trial, crucifixion, and resurrection, and about the disciples Andrew, Philip, and Thomas.

John, the Let'ters of

These three NT epistles, traditionally assigned to the writer of the Fourth Gospel and Revelation, testify that God is love and that love is the test of religion. *Second John* is written to "the elect lady and her children," probably a church; *Third John* is addressed "to the beloved Gaius."

Jo'nah, Jo'nas

(Heb. "dove") The name of 2 persons in the OT, one of whom is the central figure of the Book of Jonah.

Jo'nah, the Book of

This OT book is the story of a prophet sent by God to Nineveh. Jonah was fearful of the call and tried to flee by sea to Tarshish. During the sea voyage he was thrown overboard by his fellow passengers and swallowed by a great fish sent by God. The prophet was saved and went on to Nineveh to successfully convert the people of that city.

Jon'a•than

(Heb. "Yah has given") The name of 15 persons in the OT, one of whom was the eldest son of Saul and David's friend. To David he gave his own robe and armor. He was a man of great strength and courage. He fell, with his father and 2 brothers, at the battle of Gilboa, leaving a son 5 years old, Meribbaal or Mephibosheth. He was lamented by David in the elegy called the Song of the Bow (2 Sam. 1.17-27).

Jop'pa, Ja'pho

(Heb. "beautiful") At this seaport for Jerusalem little excavation has been possible, because the site is a rock hill on which one city after another has been built. It first appears as a city in about 1500 B.C. when it was captured by Egyptians. Rafts of cedar logs for the Temple were floated to Joppa from Lebanon. Now it has become a part of the city of Tel Aviv.

Jo'ram, Je•ho'ram

(Heb. "Yah is high") The name of 5 persons in the OT, one of whom, Jehoram, was king of Judah (849-842 B.C.).

Jor'dan

The chief river of Palestine, flowing S for 100 miles through a deep valley. Its 3 sources are at the foot of Hermon. In its course are 2 lakes, Lake Huleh and the Sea of Galilee. From the Sea of Galilee to the Dead Sea the Jordan Valley (Ghor) is 65 mi. falling from 682 to 1292 ft. below sea level. The average width of the river is not more than 30 yds., and it varies in depth from 3 ft. at the fords to 7, 8, and 10 ft. The current is very rapid. The river was miraculously crossed by the Israelites and by Elijah and Elisha. In its waters Jesus was baptized by John the Baptist.

Jo'sech
See Joseph.

Jo'seph, Jo'se•phus, Jo'sech, Jo'ses
(Heb. "may Yah add") The name of 14 persons in the Bible. Included are Joseph the son of Jacob, Joseph the husband of Mary the mother of Jesus, and Joseph of Arimathea.

1. *Joseph, husband of Mary.* A carpenter, resident of Nazareth, descended from David. It is presumed that he died in Jesus' youth because there is little mention of him after Jesus was 12.

2. *Joseph, the son of Jacob and Rachel.* He was father of Ephraim and Manasseh, and thus ancestor of the people of the Northern Kingdom. Sold into Egypt by his brothers, he was imprisoned on a false accusation by his master's wife. (A similar incident occurs in a story, written in the time of Ramses II, preserved in a papyrus now in the British Museum.) Yet his skill in interpreting dreams brought him Pharaoh's favor and the first place next to the throne. Gen 42–47 relates how, during a famine, his father and brothers came to settle in Goshen.

3. *Joseph of Arimathea.* A member of the Sanhedrin. He buried the body of Jesus in a tomb on his own property.

Josh′u·a, Jesh′u·a
(Heb. "Yah is salvation") The name of 11 persons in the OT, one of whom is Joshua, son of Nun. Of the tribe of Ephraim, he led the people into the Promised Land. He died at age 110.

Josh′u·a, the Book of
This OT book tells the story of Moses' successor as leader of the Israelites, Joshua, son of Nun, and narrates the conquest of Canaan and the division of the country among the twelve tribes of Israel.

Jo·si′ah
(Heb. "let Yah give") The son of Amon, king of Judah from 639 to 608 B.C. In the 18th year of his reign the Book of the Law was discovered and thereafter the high places throughout the country were suppressed. He was defeated and slain by Pharaoh-Neco at Megiddo. Under his sons Jehoahaz (609), Jehoiachim (608-598) and Zedekiah (597-586) the kingdom of Judah was by turns under Egyptian and Babylonian domination, till its extinction in 586 B.C.

jot
A transliteration of iota, the name of the smallest letter in the Greek alphabet; used metaphorically for the smallest thing.

Jo′tham
(Heb. "may Yah complete") The name of 3 persons in the OT, one of whom was king of Judah 742-735 B.C.

Ju′bi·lee
The final year in a cycle of 50 years brought restoration of inheritance.

Ju·dae'a, Ju'dah

See Judea.

Ju'da·iz·ers

A name given to those among the early Jewish Christians who could not believe that all that had once been conveyed to man through the Law was now made available in far greater fullness in the Gospel. Thus they insisted on circumcision as giving a man the right to believe on Jesus as Israel's Savior. The Judaizers were a dwindling body among Palestinian Christians, and they have left no real record of themselves in the New Testament. When they appear in history later on, it is under the title of Ebionites, representing, as their predecessors had done, the "poor" (Heb. *ebion*) and oppressed classes in Jewish society.

Ju'das

The name of 6 persons in the NT, one of whom was Judas Iscariot, the betrayer of Jesus.

Ju'das Mac·ca·be'us

See Maccabees.

Jude, the Let'ter of

This NT epistle designates its author as "a servant of Jesus Christ and brother of James." Its message was for Christians wherever unity was threatened by heretical teaching and where Christian doctrinal and moral standards were questioned.

Ju·de'a, Ju'dah, Ju·dae'a

The land of the Jews, a name applied sometimes to the whole land of Palestine, sometimes to the S division only. It was used in the wider sense at the close of the Captivity, most of those who returned having belonged to the ancient kingdom of Judah. Under the Romans, and in the time of Christ, the name was restricted to the S division; the N being Galilee, and the middle, Samaria; but even then it sometimes denoted the whole country. In its limited sense, it formed part of the kingdom of Herod the Great, and included part of Idumaea, or the land of Edom. As a Roman province, it was annexed to the proconsulate of Syria, and was governed by a procurator. "The wilderness of Judea," in which John began his preaching, and where the temptation of Christ took place, was the E part of Judah, near the Dead Sea, and stretching toward Jericho. It was, and is still, a dreary and desolate region.

Judg'es, the Book of

This OT book is so called because it relates of the times of various rulers, or judges, of Israel from the possession of Canaan until the time of Samuel. Also found in Judges is the recounting of the adventures of Samson.

Ju'dith

1. This Deuterocanonical book is a story that was originally in Hebrew, but is not now extant in that language. It relates that when Nebuchadnezzar's general, Holofernes, was besieging the Jewish fortress of Bethulia, the besieged were rescued from their peril by the self-sacrifice of Judith, a Jewish woman, who surrendered herself to the camp of Holofernes, and by a stratagem succeeded in cutting off Holofernes' head.

The story was probably written to inflame patriotic feeling at the time of some invasion.

2. Esau had a foreign wife named Judith.

ju'ni·per, heath

An almost leafless broom found in the Jordan Valley and the wilderness of Sinai. The Lebanon juniper is a timber-producing tree.

K

Ka'desh, Ka·desh-bar'ne·a, Mer·i·bah-ka'desh

Ancient Canaanite cities with the name Kadesh were sanctuaries. Two of them have been identified.

Kad'mon·ites

(Heb. "easterners") The people inhabiting the Syro-Arabian Desert between Palestine and the Euphrates.

Ke'nites

(Heb. "belonging to the smiths") A gypsylike nomadic or seminomadic tribe. As early as 1300 B.C., they were doing metal work in the areas they roamed over. They lost their identity shortly after 1000 B.C.

Ke'ri·oth

(Heb. "cities") The name of 2 cities in the OT. One of them, Kerioth-Hezron, has been identified with Khirbet el-Qaryatein.

Kid'ron, Ce'dron

A valley E of Jerusalem, through which an intermittent brook still flows. At one time the waters of a spring, Gihon, were allowed to flow through this valley. The stream was often used for irrigation.

Kings, First and Sec'ond
The two OT books follow the monarchy to its summit under Solomon and the nation's division, decline, and fall under Jeroboam and Rehoboam. Kings also gives an outline of the double captivity of Israel under the Assyrians and Judah under the Chaldeans.

Kir
(Heb. "wall") The name of 2 places in the OT, one of which is identified as Kerak, 11 mi. E of the Dead Sea, 17 mi. S of the Arnon.

Kir·i·ath-se'pher, Kir·jath-se'pher
(Heb. "city of the Scribe") An older name for Debir, the modern Tell Beit Mirsin, which has been partially excavated. It is possible that Abraham visited here.

Ki'shon, Ki'son
A river draining the Valley of Jezreel and the Plain of Acco, and emptying into the Mediterranean.

Kit'tim
See Chittim.

L

L

Lam·en·ta'tions
This OT book consists of five poems occasioned by the fall of Jerusalem and the Babylonian captivity. The first three elegies describe the

terrible plight of the nation, the fourth compares the past history of Zion with her present state, and the last is a prayer for compassion and deliverance.

lamp'stand

See candlestick.

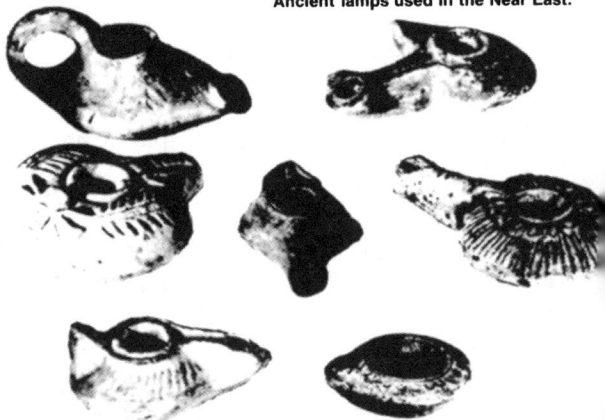

Ancient lamps used in the Near East.

La·od·i·ce'a

A city on the Lycus River in Phrygia, one of the richest in Asia. It struck its own coins, traded wisely, and was an early Christian center. When destroyed by an earthquake in A.D. 60, it was affluent enough to arrange its own reconstruction.

lap'is laz'u·li, sap'phire

Both are blue stones, lapis being semiprecious and sometimes substituted for sapphire. *See* Sapphire.

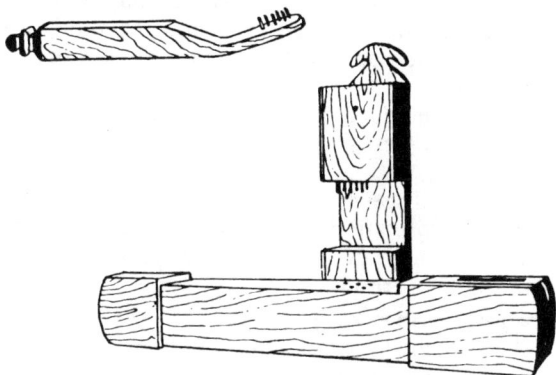

Ancient wooden lock, showing the bolt with its pins,
and also the lift key to release it

la'ver
A vessel used in ceremonial rites of purification
in the tabernacles and temples, and particularly in
Solomon's Temple at Jerusalem. The priests
washed their hands and feet in this laver before
offering sacrifices (Exod 30.18–21).

law, the
The earliest collection of laws so far discovered
is that of Ur, earlier than 2000 B.C. Several
almost equally early codes have been found, including the code of Hammurabi. All these show
evidence of being much earlier in actuality than
the incised inscriptions found and translated.
What has been called the law of Moses, found
in the Pentateuch, may also be much earlier
than its actual date of transcription. It is instruc-

tion and direction for moral, judicial, and ceremonial conduct, called the Torah by the Jewish people. The code of the Pentateuch is more humane in its judicial sections than other early codes, and much finer in its moral sections. In NT times Jesus recognized and accepted the divine origin and authority of these phases of the law. Though discussion of their extension and interpretation still continues, they are the basis of much of the code of the civilized world today. *See* Torah.

law'yers, scribes
Those skilled in the interpretation of the laws set down by Moses. *See* Scribes.

Laz'a·rus
1. Lazarus, the beggar in Jesus' account of the beggar and the rich man, was taken to Abraham's bosom when he died. But the rich man was in torment after death and he wanted his brothers to be warned of what might befall them. He was denied.

2. Lazarus of Bethany, brother of Mary and Martha, was raised to life after being four days dead. This may have been a major factor in the decision to kill Jesus: their inability to explain the raising of Lazarus was infuriating to the high priests and the Pharisees.

lead
The metal was imported into Palestine, apparently from Tyre. There are, however, mines in the Lebanon, as well as in Sinai and parts of Egypt.

Leb'a·non
(Heb. "white") A mountain range to the N of Palestine, with summits of more than 11,000 ft. For a part of the year they are snow-capped.

leeks
These are included with onions and garlic as among the good things of Egypt for which the Israelites lusted in the wilderness.

len'tils
A legume used for food; a member of the pea family.

leop'ard
A large carnivorous animal found in Palestine as late as the 20th century. The Cheetah, a hunting leopard, was also widely familiar and is found in ancient sculptures.

lep'ro·sy
The Hebrew name means "a stroke," the disease being regarded as the sorest affliction by the hand of God. Its description is given in Lev 13, 14, along with the regulations connected with it. The "botch of Egypt" was probably elephantiasis, which, it is generally agreed, was the disease that afflicted Job, and which is quite distinct from leprosy. Lepers were required to live outside the camp or city and to warn passersby with cries of "Unclean! Unclean!"

le·vi'a·than
(Heb. "coiled one") The primeval dragon, and by extension a sea monster; the crocodile. *See* Whale.

Le'vites
The persons charged with the care of the Taber-

nacle and the Temple. They embraced all the men of the tribe of Levi, exclusive of the sons of Aaron, though the latter were also Levites and could perform any Levitical service. They were set apart for this service on behalf of the children of Israel. On the settlement of Canaan they were assigned to 48 cities, scattered over the whole country, and were provided with fields for the pasture of their cattle. In David's reign they were divided into 4 classes: (1) Assistants of the priests in the work of the sanctuary; (2) Judges and Scribes; (3) Gate-keepers; (4) Musicians. Each of these classes, with the possible exception of the 2nd, was subdivided into 24 courses, or families, to serve in rotation.

Le·vit'i·cus, the Book of

This 3rd book of the OT can also be called "The Book of the Law of the Priests" as it contains very little historical matter, concerning itself with priestly legislation and the practice of the law among the people. In Leviticus much importance is placed upon Israel's separation from all heathen influences so that the nation may retain its religious purity.

Lib'er·tines, freed'men

(Lat. "freedmen") These were probably descendants of Jews who had been taken to Rome or elsewhere by Pompey as prisoners of war and had afterward received their freedom there. They did not speak Aramaic, then the language of Jerusalem, and separate synagogues for them were established.

lice

Lice were sent upon the Egyptians as the third plague.

lign·al'oe, al'oes

Lignum aloes, or wood of aloes. *See* aloes.

lig'ure, ja'cinth

This is the gem generally called in Greek lyncurion, from a singular notion as to its origin, which is identified with the true jacinth.

lil'y

This may have meant the scarlet martegon lily or the scarlet anemone, or have been used poetically for the lion; a beautiful flower.

li'on

Mentioned in the OT about 130 times, the animal was well known throughout W Asia as late as 500 B.C. The lion, Judah's emblem, was in all lands the symbol of royal power and strength. It was taken by pitfalls in its tracks, or by nets.

liz'ard

(Heb. "clinger"?) A reptile with scaly body, long tail, and usually 4 legs. A number of species occur in Palestine, including geckoes, skinks, and chameleons, and larger spiny lizards.

L

lo'custs

These insects are often referred to, and under 9 different names:

1. *Arbeh,* generally and rightly translated "locust." The record of the 8th plague in Egypt gives a true account of a typical severe invasion of locusts; an E wind brought them from the other side of the isthmus of Suez, and a W wind

hurled them back into the Red Sea, where they perished. They are placed among the clean creatures.

2. *Sal'am*, occurring once only, and translated "bald locust." The word seems to have the same root as *sela*, which means rock; hence we may think of certain species of grasshoppers, which delight in basking on sun-exposed rocks, and translate the word "rock locust."

3. *Chargol*. In the vernacular, these are called katydids or long-horned grasshoppers.

4. *Chagab*, generally used for and translated "grasshoppers," many of which are much smaller than locusts.

5. *Gazam*, translated "palmerworm," is interpreted either as the locust in its larval stage or as the larva of butterflies or moths. "Palmerworm" should not apply to locusts.

6. *Yelek*, very difficult to interpret, the more so since there is no evidence that the different authors meant the same creature. It is translated "cankerworm" and caterpillar." Etymologically, the word means a creature that licks up the grass. It is evidently intended to express some insect pest.

7. *Tzelatzal*. The word *tzelatzal* means a tinkling, musical instrument, and is hence applied to a creature able to produce musical sounds. Thus the author may have used it as the name of one of the grasshoppers, the chirping notes of which are frequently loud enough to be heard at some distance, or for the well-

known cicada, which is found in abundance all around the Mediterranean.

8. *Gob* appears several times, and is translated "grasshoppers"; it cannot be referred to any particular kind.

9. *Chasil,* generally mentioned together with the locust, and therefore believed to signify the locust in its larval stage. But in some versions it is translated "caterpillar." *See* grasshopper.

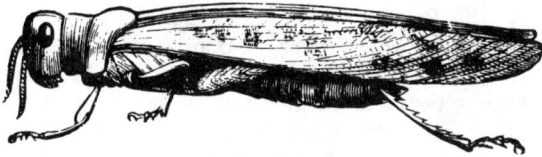

Egyptian locust

Lord's Prayer

The model prayer which our Lord taught His disciples. According to the text of Luke it consists of 5 petitions, according to that of Matthew of 6 (or 7). The Reformed churches count 6; 3 with "Thy," and 3 with "our"; the Roman Catholics and Lutherans 7, regarding "Lead us not into temptation" and "Deliver us from evil" as separate petitions. The concluding doxology (occurring only in Matthew, and omitted in some versions), is wanting in the best MSS., and is a later addition, based on 1 Chron 29.11, and 2 Tim 4.18. It accords with the first 3 petitions.

Lord's Sup'per

(Cor 11.20), called also "breaking of bread" (Acts 2.42), "cup of blessing," "communion of the blood of Christ," and "of the body of Christ" (1 Cor 10.16), and "the Lord's table" (10.21). It is a holy ordinance, which Christ initiated as the last meal (the Passover) with His disciples, on the night before His death, and appointed to be observed in remembrance of Him. In it, by the giving and receiving of bread and wine, Christ's death is showed forth "till He come." As the Passover commemorated Israel's deliverance from the "house of bondage," and election to be a covenant-people, the Lord's Supper marks the establishment of a new covenant in His blood, His death being the foundation of a new relation of His church to God, and of the communion of His people with one another.

Lot

The nephew of Abraham, who came with Abraham to Canaan. The story of Lot is found in Gen 11.27–14.29; 19.

love ap'ple

The mandrake, a perennial herb, related to the poisonous nightshade. It is superstitiously considered an aphrodisiac.

Lu'ci·fer

(Lat. "light bringer") The son of the morning was a name applied by the prophet to the king of Babylon in his pride and splendor and glory before his fall, when he said, "I will ascend into heaven, I will exalt my throne above the stars of God" (Is 14.12-13).

Luke

A Gentile, a physician, an educated man, familiar with the E Mediterranean and adjacent countries, who in Acts appears as the companion of Paul from Troas to Philippi, where he probably remained from A.D. 52 to 58, rejoining the Apostle at that place, and continuing with him to the time when the narration closes (A.D. 58-63). In 2 Tim. 4.11 he is referred to as being with Paul. Hence the evangelist must have been in Palestine during the 2 years of Paul's imprisonment at Caesarea (A.D. 58-60).

Luke, the Gos'pel according to

This NT book, the 3rd Gospel, was written by "The beloved physician," the companion of the apostle Paul. Only in Luke are found the Magnificat, the story of the birth of John the Baptist, the Christmas story of the shepherds, the parables of the good Samaritan, the lost sheep, and the prodigal son, and the great hymns—the *Gloria in Excelsis* and *Nunc Dimittis*. Jesus is presented as the compassionate Savior, healer, redeemer, and friend of the weak. From this Gospel comes a special feeling of the mercy of God as Jesus made men understand it.

lute

An instrument resembling the harp and the cithern; examples have been found of the period of 1500 B.C.

LXX

See Septuagint.

lye

See Nitre.

lyre

An early stringed instrument found in Egyptian and Assyrian relief, the "harp" played by David. Played especially in the Temple by the Levites.

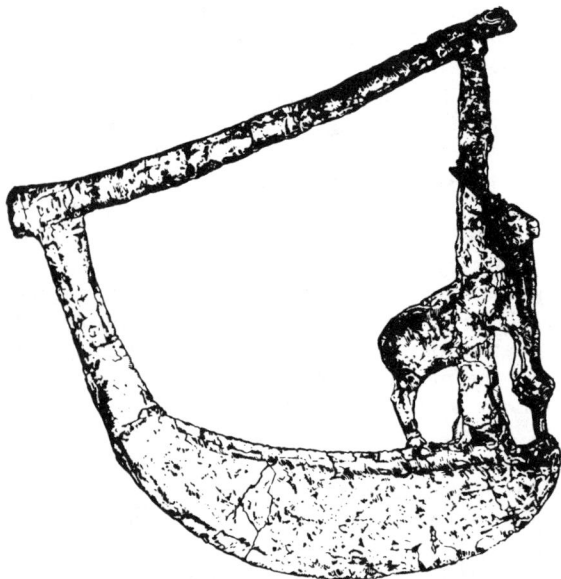

Lyre frame of silver, from Ur, dated previous to the time of Abraham

M

Mac′ca·bees

The family of priestly descent that freed the Jewish people from the Syrian yoke. The name Makkaba ("hammer") belongs properly to Judas, the third of the five sons of Mattathias, who from his father's death in 166 B.C. to his own death at the battle of Elasa or Adasa in 161 led the defenders of their country and faith in one of the most heroic struggles in history. His work was completed by his brothers, who founded the Asmonaean Dynasty.

Mac·e·do′ni·a

In NT times, the northern Roman province of Greece, the southern being Achaia. Paul was summoned thither by the vision of the "man of Macedonia" and he visited it a 2nd time. Philippi was one of its chief cities, and there Lydia was converted.

Ma′gi

In the NT, the wise men from the East who came to worship the infant Christ. The name Magos is also given to Elymas in Acts 13.6, 8, and is there translated "sorcerer"; and to Simon who "used sorcery" (Acts 8.9).

Mal′a·chi

(Heb. "My messenger") An OT prophet.

Mal′a·chi, the Book of

The last book of the OT belongs to the period of Nehemiah. The prophet's message is to the priests and the people, charging them with indifference, doubt, and immorality. Malachi tells of the coming day of the Lord and closes the book with a prophecy of John the Baptist.

mal'low
Probably the shrubby orache, eaten only when nothing else is available.

Ma·nas'seh
(Heb. "one who causes to forget") The name of 2 persons in the OT, one the eldest son of Joseph and ancestor of one of the 12 tribes; the other was Judah's king (687-642 B.C.).

Ma·nas'seh, Prayer of
It is mentioned in the statement by the Chronicler, 2 Chron 33.18, 19. The extant Prayer of Manasseh found in the Apocrypha is a noble monument of devotion. The early Christian church placed it as one of the 9 canticles at the head of the Psalter.

man'drake
See Love apple.

man'na
(Heb. "What is that?") The food supplied to the Israelites in the wilderness. Some studies in the Sinai region theorize that it is the honeydew secretion of two scale insects on the tamarisk bushes abundant there, very sweet and high in carbohydrates.

mar'ble
The name is properly applied to a completely crystalline limestone, such as is used for statuary, but is commonly extended to any orna-

mental limestone that can be polished. In Palestine, probably the latter was meant.

Mar'che·wan

A name of the 8th month of the Hebrew year. It is also called Bul.

Mark, John Mark

He was the son of Mary, at whose house in Jerusalem the early Christians seem to have found a home. He was a cousin of Barnabas, and the attendant of the 2 Christian preachers in Paul's first missionary journey. But he became the occasion of sharp contention between Paul and Barnabas in consequence of his leaving them at Perga. Afterward, however, he was with the Apostle Paul during his first imprisonment at Rome. The Apostle Peter refers to Mark as with him when he wrote his 1st epistle, probably at Babylon. Evidently the evangelist made a journey to the E about A.D. 63, and he was at Ephesus with Timothy shortly before the death of Paul. Reliable details of his later life are wanting. He is spoken of as the interpreter of Peter, and, according to tradition, was the founder of the church at Alexandria. His Gospel may have been written at Rome, between A.D. 63 and 66.

M

Mark, the Gos'pel according to

The earliest of the Gospels, this NT book contains much of the teaching of Peter. This Gospel presents Jesus as the man of power, the strong and active Son of God; its climax is reached when Peter makes his great confession, "You are the Christ."

Ma'ry

The name of 7 persons in the NT, one of them the mother of Jesus. Another Mary was the sister of Lazarus; a third is the mother of James the Younger; and a fourth, Mary Magdalene.

Mas'o·retes

Down to the close of the 5th century A.D., the tradition of the accepted pronunciation of the bare consonantal text of the OT was kept alive by the oral teaching of the Rabbis and by the recitation of the Scriptures in the synagogues. The reduction to writing of this exegetical tradition was the work of the scholars called the Masoretes, (from Masora, "tradition"), whose chief center was the Rabbinical school of Tiberias. They took great pains that the texts should be kept entire, for this purpose counting up the number of words, and even the number of letters in the different books, noting expressions that occurred but once or rarely, drawing attention to peculiar modes of writing, and the like. One great service rendered by the Masoretes was their devising a system of dots and strokes (vowel points), which are placed above, below, or in the heart of the consonants, and denote precisely how the words were read by the scholars of the time. These are regarded as forming no part of the sacred text, and the Pentateuch rolls used in the Synagogue are written in the bare consonants as originally received. Closely connected with the vowel system is the system of accents, which indicate the manner in which the words and clauses were separated or conjoined, and also form a kind of musical notation, according to which the Scriptures are to be melodiously recited. The text, with this array of symbols, is called the Masoretic text; and it gives us what was the traditional reading at the time the work was accomplished.

The Masoretic text, with its complete equipment, cannot be placed earlier than the 7th century of the Christian era. But it gives us a tradition reaching back to a much earlier time; and it is a cause of thankfulness that, in the handing down of the text, the Masoretes did not allow themselves to deviate in the smallest details from what they had received. There remain in the text, as they have handed it down, evident indications of what had been slips of the pen or mistakes of the eye of the transcribers, but the Masoretes allowed even these to stand, contenting themselves with drawing attention to their presence.

mas·se'ba

A sacred pillar.

Mat'thew

(Heb. "gift of Yah") Also called "Levi the son of Alphaeus." When called to become a disciple he was a publican, or tax gatherer, probably a collector of tolls and custom duties at the Sea of Galilee. His call is narrated in the 3 Gospels, but while he refers to the feast that Mark and Luke distinctly place at his house, he makes no allusion to that fact. Papias and Irenaeus, writing in the 2nd century, state that

M

Matthew wrote in Hebrew (Aramaic). The earliest citations, some of them in works of the earlier half of the 2nd century, give the exact words of the Greek Gospel we now have, and no certain traces of a previous Aramaic Gospel have been discovered. If there was an Aramaic original, it was superseded very soon by a Greek version. The very early date often assigned (A.D. 45) may be correct if applied to an Aramaic original; but the Greek Gospel we have may have been written about A.D. 60.

Mat'thew, the Gos'pel according to

This first NT book has been pre-eminently the Gospel of the church. It tells us of God's love for Israel and of the fulfillment in Christ of God's promise to the nation. It gives the complete story of Jesus' ministry, death, and resurrection. The Sermon on the Mount, and some of the most precious of Jesus' parables are contained in this Gospel.

meals

In Palestine there were two meals, one late in the morning and the other, the chief one, in the evening.

meas'ures

Bath (liquid) = 5½ gallons.

Cor (liquid or dry) = 10 baths (liquid) = 55 gals. (dry).

Cubit (length) = 21.8 inches English (or 20.24 inches for the ordinary cubit).

Ephah (dry) = ½ bushel.

Hin (liquid) = 4 quarts.

Homer (dry) = 5.16 bushels.

Kab (dry) = 1.16 quarts.
Log (liquid or dry) = 0.67 pint.
Omer (dry) = 2.09 quarts.
Seah (dry) = ⅔ peck.

Medes

An Aryan or Indo-European people who inhabitated the country to the SW of the Caspian, whence they extended S to the Persian Gulf. One of the offshoots was the tribe of Persians. Called also Madai.

Me·gid'do, Me·gid'don, Ar·ma·ged'don

A Canaanite and later Israelite city identified as the modern Tell el-Mutesellim, overlooking the Plain of Esdraelon, 20 mi. SSE of Haifa. As an inhabited area it has a history of more than 3500 years. Both Egyptians and people from the E destroyed it. Thut-mose III of Egypt about 1450 B.C., Tiglath-pileser III the Assyrian in 733 B.C., and Neco of Egypt in 609 B.C. destroyed it completely. During its long history it has been a walled city, a royal chariot city, a city of great splendor, the site of many battles. It is believed to be the place of Armageddon, the final struggle. *See* Armageddon.

Mel·chiz'e·dek, Melchisedec (KJV)

M

(trad. "King of righteousness") A worshiper of the Supreme God, to whom, as priest and king of Salem or Jerusalem, Abraham gave tithes. In Heb 7 he is shown to be a type of Christ.

mel'on

A fruit known to them in Egypt for which the Israelites longed when in the wilderness. Both muskmelons and watermelons are common in Egypt.

Mer·i·bah-ka'desh

See Kadesh.

Mer'o·dach-bal'a·dan, Ber'o·dach-bal'a·dan

Ruler of a Chaldean tribe and twice (721-710, 704 B.C.) king of Babylon (Jer 50.2).

Me'sha

The name of 2 persons and a place in the OT, and of the king of Moab who erected the Moabite Stone, which chronicled his story.

Me'shach

The Babylonian name of one of the friends of Daniel. *See* Shadrach.

Mes·o·po·ta'mi·a

The land between the rivers, the Tigris and the Euphrates.

Mes·si'ah, Mes·si'as

(Heb. the "Anointed," same as Gr. *Christos*) Though in the OT sometimes applied to such divinely appointed agents as the high priest, the prophets, and even King Cyrus (Is 45.1), chiefly designates the promised Deliverer and Saviour whom prophecy foretold, and in whom all the promises of God are fulfilled.

Mi'cah

(Heb. "who is like Yah?") Micah the prophet, a contemporary of Isaiah.

Mi'cah, the Book of

The prophecy of the fourth in the great quartet of eighth-century B.C. prophets, with Amos, Hosea, and Isaiah, who preached against the idolatrous and unjust nations of their generation. Micah's message was stern and uncompromising; judgment was to come soon for Judah.

Mi'chael

(Heb. "who is like God?") One of the archangels.

Mid'i·an·ites

A tribe living in NW Arabia, descendants of Keturah and Abraham. They were nomads and traders with Egypt, and pillaged the Israelites until conquered by Gideon.

Mil'com

See Molech.

mill

The handmill consisted of 2 stones, between which the grain was ground. A rectangular and slightly concave stone might be rubbed over a larger stone, or 2 round stones, the lower convex and the upper concave, might have grain for grinding poured through a hole in the center of the top stone. These mills were used by women in the home. Larger round millstones turned on a flat lower stone by animal power were community enterprises. No part of a handmill could be taken for debt.

mil'let

The smallest of the grass seeds grown for food; usually mixed with other seeds or grains.

mil'lo

A part of the fortification of Jerusalem, erected by David.

mi'na

See Weights.

M

Mi'nor Proph'ets
  The last 12 books of the OT. Because of their brevity, they are frequently called the minor prophets.

mint
  (Gr. "sweet odor") An herb, the oil of which was used as a condiment and as medicine. Several species are found in Palestine. The Pharisees required the tithing even of mint, but neglected law and justice, mercy and faith.

Mint

mir'a·cle
(Lat. "wonderful thing") Defined as an event, whether natural or supernatural, in which one sees an act or revelation of God.

mite
See Money.

Miz'pah, Miz'peh
(Heb. "watchtower") The name of 4 towns and 1 region in the OT; 2 towns and the region have been tentatively identified.

Miz'ra·im
The Hebrew word for Egypt; it also applies to a land of Musri, from which Shalmaneser III got double-humped camels. Solomon imported horses from a place of this name.

Mo'ab·ites
A people allied to the Israelites, settled from before the time of Moses SE of the Dead Sea. Like the Ammonites, from whom they were separated by the river Arnon, they were descendants of Lot, and mortal enemies of Israel. They were subdued by Saul and David, and after Ahab's death cast off the yoke of the N kingdom. To this period belongs the Moabite Stone. Jeroboam II again made them tributary.

Mo'ab·ite Stone
In 1868 an inscription was found among the ruins of Dibon, giving an account by the Moabite king Mesha of his successful revolt from Samaria, and of his buildings in Moab. "Omri, king of Israel, oppressed Moab many days, for Chemosh was angry with his land." Then Mesha revolted in the time of Ahab. He over-

M

threw the Israelites, took Medeba, Ataroth, Jahaz, and Nebo, where there had been an altar to "Yahweh" (Jehovah), and he rebuilt Korkhah, Aroer, Bezer, and other fortresses. It is clear from 2 Kings 3.5 that the chief successes of Mesha were gained after Ahab's death. The language of the inscription hardly differs from Hebrew.

mole

(Heb. "digger"?) The moles of Is 2.20 perhaps included the rat, ground squirrel, and similar animals. The U. S. mole is unknown in Palestine, but the mole-rat is very abundant.

Mo'lech, Mo'loch, Mil'com, Ath'ter

A deity to whom human sacrifices were made, and worshiped by Ammonites, Edomites, Moabites, and others. The Valley of Hinnom, outside Jerusalem, was a place of sacrifice to this god.

mon'ey

In the sense of stamped coin, money did not exist in Israel before the Exile. Of coined money, an invention of the Greeks, there is some trace in Western Asia in the 7th century B.C. in the Greek colonies and in Lydia. Gold and silver earlier were "weighed to" the seller by the buyer. The name of the common unit, the shekel, means "weight" (cf. English pound sterling; also Old French livre, and Italian lira, from Latin libra, "a pound"). The pieces of metal were in the form of bars (cf. the "wedge" of 50 shekels' weight in Josh 7.21), larger pieces in that of rings, as the Hebrew name for talent

Silver quarter-shekel

Copper coin of Cyprus

Daric

("circle") shows. The weighing of ring money is represented on the Egyptian monuments. The balance and the weights (of stone) were carried along with the precious metal in a bag attached to the girdle.

Recent investigations have proved that the ratio of the value of gold to that of silver fixed in Babylon and Assyria, 1:13½, prevailed over all Western Asia (in Greece it was 1:12). The whole monetary system of the Hebrews, as of their neighbors, was based on the Babylonian system of weights. The Babylonian weight-talent was equal to 60 minas of 60 shekels each; but the Babylonian money-talent was equal to 60 minas of 50 shekels each, or 3000 shekels. The unit, the shekel, was the same in both.

Darius I, Darius Hystaspes, extended the circulation of coins, but a gold coin called the daric was used earlier by King Cyrus (550-530 B.C.). After the Exile, Persian money was current. After the fall of the Persian monarchy, talents and drachmas came in. Simon Maccabaeus struck (141 B.C.) silver and bronze coins, of which a number are still extant, but the Greek money was still current, and in the time of our Lord they counted by drachmas and staters. The smallest copper coin in use is translated mite.

COINS OF THE BIBLE

Assarion, a Roman bronze coin, 1/10 denarius to 1/20 denarius. *See penny.*

Aureus, a Roman gold coin. Its weight was changed several times.

Mite of Herod the Great

Shekel of the sanctuary

Beka, Bekah, half a shekel, 0.201 ounce.

Daric or *Dram,* a Persian gold coin, 8.424 grams.

Denarius, a Roman silver coin, 3.8 grams.

Drachma, a Greek silver coin, nearly equal to the Roman denarius.

Dram. See daric.

Gerah, 1/20 shekel, 8.71 grams.

Gold, the Roman aureus = 25 denarii, was of pure gold, and weighed 126¼ grains.

Lepton, the smallest Greek bronze coin; possibly 1/100 drachma. *See mite.*

Mite, the smallest Jewish coin.

Money, pieces of, in Gen 33.19; Job 42.11; Josh 24.32, are of unknown value. In the NT, piece of money, Gr. stater (only in Mt 17.27; R. V. shekel), a silver coin, the Attic silver tetradrachma (four drachmas), officially tariffed by Pompey 63 B.C. for purposes of exchange, at 4 denarii.

Penny in the NT represents a Roman silver coin, the denarius. It was the daily wage of a laborer or of a common soldier in the time of our Lord.

Pound (only occurring in Lk 19.13-25) is the mina = 100 drachmas.

Shekel (Heb. "weight," only in OT), 0.403 ounce. The "holy" shekel, mentioned in parts of Exodus, Leviticus, and Numbers, means the full weight shekel, as contrasted with that which had deteriorated in weight.

Denarius with image and superscription of
Tiberius Caesar

Silver half-shekel of Year 1

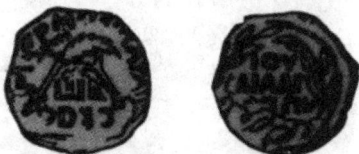

Procurator's copper coin

Silver coin of Vespasian, commemorating the
capture of Jerusalem

Silver, piece of. Here probably shekels are meant. In the NT "piece of silver" represents the Gr. drachma or the silver shekel.

Silverlings. Silver shekels.

Talent, about 75 pounds.

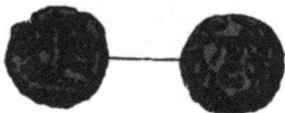

Copper coin of Herod Antipas, Tetrarch of Galilee

Silver Drachma of Alexander the Great found at
the Treasury, Persepolis, Iran

mon'ey chang'ers

The money changers at the Temple sat in the court of the Gentiles, and were not allowed within the inner precincts or naos. Here they acted as bankers, and gave Jewish money in exchange for foreign, as only Jewish money could be used to pay the Temple tax. The practices of the money changers must have been so bad as to warrant their expulsion by our Lord, who "overthrew the tables of the money changers."

Weighing money

M

Mor′de·cai

The name of 2 persons in the OT, one of them the important character of the Book of Esther.

Mo·ri′ah

A region near Beer-Sheba, mentioned in the OT. Also, a rocky hill of Jerusalem N of the City of David, and the site of the Temple.

Mo′ses

The great deliverer and law-giver of Israel was the son of Amram and Jochebed, of the tribe of Levi, and younger brother of Miriam and Aaron. Born during the oppression of the Israelites in Egypt, he was placed while an infant child in an ark of bulrushes among the reeds of the river Nile, where he was found by the daughter of Pharaoh. Brought up in Pharaoh's house, he became learned in "all the wisdom of the Egyptians." In his 40th year he fled to Midian, "fearing the wrath of the king" for his killing an Egyptian whom he had found ill-treating a Hebrew. In Midian he married Zipporah, daughter of a priest and sheikh, and lived 40 years. Then God revealed Himself to Moses as Jehovah in a bush that burned and was not consumed, and commissioned him to return to Egypt and be the deliverer of Israel. After 10 miracles of judgment or "plagues" wrought by Moses, the greatest and last of these being the death of the first-born, Pharaoh consented, and the children of Israel set forth for Canaan. Thenceforward for 40 years he was their leader through the wilderness; at Sinai, where he received the law from Heaven; at Kadesh; and in the land of Moab, where he died, after viewing the promised land from the top of Pisgah. Moses, "the mediator of the old covenant," is one of the greatest figures in history. He made the children of Israel a nation, and established the national life of Israel on the basis of a religious covenant that determined the whole future of that people and of the world.

moth

(Heb. "consumer") The moth mentioned in the Bible is the clothes moth, of which several species are very destructive to fur and wool and the garments made of them. It is only the larvae that feed upon the hairs. In Is 51.8 we read, "For the moth shall eat them up like a garment, and the worm (Heb. sas) shall eat them like wool"; the word sas, translated "worm," is interpreted as the larva.

mourn'ing

Signs of mourning were: rending the outer garments, wearing sackcloth, strewing earth or ashes, cutting or shaving beard or hair, fasting, and in some cases, even cutting the hands and the body.

mouse

Doubtless a generic term, including all the small rodents. The mouse was forbidden as food by the Mosaic law.

M

mul'ber·ry, syc'a·mine, bal'sam

The black mulberry is common in Palestine. The Heb. word has also been translated as sycamine and as balsam.

A bough of the mulberry tree

mur'der·ers

See Assassins.

mur'rain

An infectious disease of animals.

mu'sic

According to 1 Chron 15.17, David, credited as the originator of liturgical music, instituted an orchestra, with 3 leaders: Heman, Asaph, Ethan or Jeduthun, all of them Levites. These pioneers founded schools of musical performance. The instruments played were percussion, cymbals and timbrels or tambourines; stringed psalteries and harps; wind instruments, the pipe and the trumpet or cornet. There was antiphonal singing by Temple choirs and singing by the congregations.

Ancient musical instruments

M

The Temple priests used trumpets and cornets on special occasions, and the priestly family made up an orchestra as well.

mus'tard
An annual plant with very small seeds. It grows to a considerable size in Palestine.

Mustard

myrrh, per′fume

A general term for fragrant gums or resins from various trees and shrubs, most frequently the rockrose, the ladanum. It was an article of commerce as early as the 2nd millennium B.C.

myr′tle

A shrub indigenous to Western Asia and common on hillsides in Palestine, flourishing especially by watercourses. It has dark glossy leaves, marked with transparent dots, the result of the presence of a volatile aromatic oil. The flowers are small, white, and fragrant, and when dried are used as a perfume.

N

Na′a·man

(Heb. "pleasantness") A Syrian army commander, healed of leprosy by Elisha.

Na′hum, Na′um

The name of a person of the OT and one of the NT. Nahum of the OT and prophet of the Book of Nahum was born at Elkosh in SW Judah and prophesied in the period between 633 and 612 B.C.

Na′hum, the Book of

This OT book consists of two poems. The prophet tells of the fall of Nineveh, the capital of the Assyrian nation. God is depicted as revengeful to those who conspire against Him. The book of Nahum also contains a classic rebuke against warfare and militarism.

N

Na'in

(Heb. "pleasant") A town of SW Galilee, now called Nein, on the NW side of Nebi Dahi and 2 mi. SW of Endor.

nard

See Spikenard.

Na'than

(Heb. "gift") The court prophet who denounced David for planning Uriah's death and stealing his wife; he also assisted in securing the throne for Solomon.

Na·than'a·el

(Heb. "gift of God") A man of Cana of Galilee, often identified with Bartholomew.

Naz'a·reth

(Heb. "watchtower") The village in Lower Galilee where Jesus was brought up. It is not mentioned in the OT. It is now a flourishing town. The "brow of the hill" is probably the cliff to the N.

Naz'i·rites

(Heb. "one consecrated") These were not members of a party or brotherhood, but individuals "separated" to God's special service by a personal vow of longer or shorter duration. Of this nature was probably the vow of the men named in Acts 21.23-26, and even of Paul (Acts 18.18). The typical Nazirite of the NT is John the Baptist.

Ne'bo

The name of a Babylonian deity, and of 2 towns mentioned in the OT, one probably Kirbeh Mèkhayyet, 5 mi. SW of Heshbon, and the other Nuba, 15 mi. SW of Jerusalem.

Ne'bo, Mount
Probably a mountain of the Abarim range, modern Jebel en-Neba, 2740 ft. above sea level, 12 mi. E of the mouth of the Jordan River.

Neb·u·chad·nez'zar, Neb·u·chad·rez'zar
(Akkad. "Nabu protect my boundary stone") King of Babylonia for 43 years, he records in an inscription his defeat of the Pharaoh Amasis in 567 B.C., verifying the prophecy of Jeremiah (43.10-13); and a contract tablet, dated in his 40th year, proves that he had by that time conquered Tyre, confirming Ezek (28.7-14).

Ne·he·mi'ah
(Heb. "Yah has comforted") The name of 3 persons in the OT, one of whom was the restorer (with Ezra) of Judaism after the Babylonian exile and cupbearer to the Persian king Artaxerxes I, who gave him permission to return with a colony to Jerusalem in 445 B.C. Appointed governor of Judea, he rebuilt the city walls in spite of the opposition of the Samaritans and others, and organized the service of God, returning to Persia in 430.

Ne·he·mi'ah, the Book of
Ezra and Nehemiah are companion OT books. *Nehemiah* (or *Second Book of Ezra*) gives an account of the rebuilding of Jerusalem and of the efforts to bring religious reform to the people, covering the history of the Jews from the Exile to the time of Darius II.

N

net'works

See cotton.

New Je·ru'sa·lem

See Jerusalem, New.

Nic·o·de'mus

(Gr. "conqueror of the people") A member of the Sanhedrin, who came at night to talk with Jesus; he provided the spices for and helped to embalm the body of Jesus.

Nic·o·la'i·tans, Nic·o·la'i·tanes

The name of a sect of Gentile Christians in Ephesus and Pergamum, who rejected the decision of the Jerusalem council with regard to food, and its prohibition of unchastity.

Nile

The great fertilizing river of Egypt. The name, which means "dark" or "blue," is not found in the Bible, but it is understood to be referred to as Shihor or the black stream and as "the river." It is formed by 2 rivers: the White Nile, which flows from the Victoria Nyanza; and the Blue Nile, which flows from the Abyssinian Mountains. These streams unite at Khartoum. To the annual overflowing of the Nile, caused by periodic rains in the southern regions around its sources, Egypt owes its fertility. Below Cairo the river is divided into channels through the Deltas. The names and locations of these shift and the precise patterns in antiquity are not known.

Nim'rod

A legendary hero of the Mesopotamian region. The legends may have grown around the Babylonian war god Ninurta, or a historical figure, the Assyrian king Tukulti-Ninurta (1246-1206 B.C.), the first Assyrian to rule over all Babylonia. Nimrod son of Cush has the legendary greatness.

Nin'e·veh

The later capital of Assyria after the kingdom had been extended north along the Tigris from Assur, the great city on the Upper Tigris, which has yielded almost a complete monumental history of Assyria. An inscription of the Akkad Dynasty (23rd to 21st century B.C.) has been found

Winged bull from the palace of Sargon near Nineveh

N

in the excavations. It was destroyed about 612
B.C. by the allied Medes, Persians, and Baby-
lonians, after having been ruined by the
Scythians.

Nip'pur
A city about 100 mi. S of Baghdad, founded
around 4000 B.C.

Ni'san
The 1st month of the Hebrew year. Also called
Abib. It falls in March-April.

ni'tre, lye
Native sodium carbonate, nitre, is found in
Egypt about 50 mi. W of Cairo. The reference
in Prov 25.20 and Jer 2.22, a substance used for
cleaning, may be potassium carbonate, which in
Palestine could be made from wood ashes. The
addition of vinegar would destroy its action.

No'ah, No'e
Tenth generation from Adam, son of Lamech,
and a righteous man, whose story is told in Gen
6–9. To Noah God gave the promise after the
Flood that never again would he send such a
catastrophe, and the rainbow was declared the
reminder of His promise. *See* Flood.

Noph
The city of Memphis in Egypt.

Num'bers, the Book of
The 4th book of the OT, it is a continuation of
Exodus, recording the stay of the Israelites in
the wilderness of Sinai until their arrival at
Moab. The title of the book is derived from the
two numberings of the people recorded here.

O

oak, ter'e·binth

Three species of oak are found in Palestine. The terebinth is now identified as distinct from the oak. Symbolism of the oak includes long life and grandeur.

O·ba·di'ah

The name of 11 persons in the OT.

O·ba·di'ah, the Book of

This is the shortest book of the OT, containing only one chapter. In it is given a prophetic interpretation of a great calamity that has already occurred in Edom and a prediction of a universal judgment.

oil tree

This term can include the olive, wild olive, oleaster, and some pines.

ol'ive

Grafted on wild stock, the olive is extensively cultivated in Palestine for its valuable fruit and oil. The cherubim, the doors of the oracle, and the doorposts of the Temple were made of its finely grained wood.

Ol'ives, Mount of; Ol'i·vet, the Mount called

A mountain with 3 summits E of Jerusalem; the highest summit, sometimes called Mount Scopus, is 2963 ft. Gethsemane is on its lower slope. The Mount of Olives is closely associated with the last days of the life of Jesus.

o·me'ga

The last letter in the Greek alphabet, used in

Revelation as a title for Christ as the One in whom all things find their consummation.

Om'ri

(Heb. "worshiper of Yah") The name of 4 persons in the OT, one of whom was king of Israel 876-968 B.C.

O·ni'as

The name of 5 priests, 2 of whom were high priests. The family descended from Zadok, appointed high priest by Solomon.

on'y·cha

An ingredient, possibly obtained from marine mollusks, of incense to be burned on the altar.

o'nyx

A chalcedony with bands of alternate milk-white and black. It is sometimes translated as a color rather than black.

O'phir

A place from which gold was obtained. The location has been placed in India, Africa, and Arabia; it seems probable that it was on the coast of Somaliland. The imports from Ophir, other than gold, seem characteristically African, such as monkeys and ivory.

or'gan, pipe

A pipe or perforated wind instrument, perhaps in a group or cluster.

or'na·ments

A list of feminine ornaments is given in Is 3.18-24. They included rings for the fingers, the ears, and the nose; bangles round the arms and the ankles; bracelets and necklaces; pomander boxes, and mirrors. Cosmetics were also

used, both to blacken the nails and the eyelids,
and to color the cheeks (2 Kings 9.30; Ezek
23.40).

Egyptian bracelets

ouch'es
Settings for jewels.

P

Pa·dan-a'ram, Pad·dan-a'ram
The area in what is now S central Turkey, including the city of Haran, now Harran.
Pal'es·tine
The Greek and Roman name for Canaan, together with the country of Jordan occupied by
the Jews (the Bible itself confines this name to
the territory of the Philistines). Palestine is 140
mi. long, 40 to 50 mi. broad, some 8500 sq. mi.
in area: about the size of Massachusetts or of
Wales. It is shut off from Egypt by 100 mi. of
desert; has the Arabian desert on the E, and the
Mediterranean on the W; and is bounded on
the N by the mountain chains of Lebanon and

Anti-Lebanon. Palestine lies midway between the valleys of the Euphrates and the Nile, two of the earliest seats of civilization and of empire. The traffic between Mesopotamia and Egypt passed through it. Of these empires Palestine was the battlefield down to 500 B.C. Then others followed: the Persians under Cambyses, Greeks under Alexander, Seleucus and the Ptolemies, the Romans under Pompey, the Parthians, the Romans again and again, then in A.D. 634 the Arabs, in the 11th century the Turks and Crusaders, in the 13th and 14th, the Mongols, and in the 19th, Napoleon.

Israel came originally from the desert, and Midianites, Ishmaelites, Amalekites, Arabs, and other Semitic tribes kept pouring into the land; hence the population is in the main Semitic to this day.

The kingdom of Herod the Great embraced all the country won by the tribes under Joshua, except the tribe of Asher in the N, and a small part in the SW. It included: (1) W of Jordan, Galilee, Samaria, Judea, and Idumea; (2) E of Jordan, Perea, Gaulanitis, Auranitis, and Trachonitis, with Decapolis (part in Perea, part in Gaulanitis). The part E of Jordan thus comprehended the ancient kingdoms of Moab and Ammon; the earlier divisions of Gilead (from the Dead Sea to the Yarmuk), and Bashan (a volcanic plateau 2000 ft. above the sea), extending from the Yarmuk to Hermon; and the regions of Golan, E of the Sea of Galilee, and Hauran, still farther E.

Palestine is laid down from N to E in 4 long lines: the Maritime Plain, the Western (or Central) Range, the Jordan Valley, and the Eastern Range. Palestine W of Jordan is an upland carved out of masses of limestone, 2000 to 3000 ft. above the sea. The Ghor, or great trench of the Jordan Valley, descends from ocean level at Huleh to 682 ft. lower at the Sea of Galilee, and to 1292 ft. at the Dead Sea. The Western Range is broken by the Plain of Esdraelon, which opens a way from the Maritime Plain to the Jordan Valley. At its S end it declines into a broad plateau named the Negev, or Parched Land. The lower hills, known as the Shephelah, are between Judea and the Maritime Plain, which, farther N, is broken by Carmel. Thus the leading features of the country are: (1) the Maritime Plain, interrupted by (2) Carmel; (3) the Low Hills or Shephelah; (4) the Western Range, cut in two by (5) Esdraelon, and running S into the (6) Negev; (7) the Jordan Valley; (8) the Eastern Range.

The rivers of Palestine are the Jordan with its lakes, Huleh (Waters of Merom) and Gennesaret (Sea of Galilee), and its E tributaries, the Yarmuk and the Jabbok; the Arnon, flowing into the Dead Sea; and the Kishon, into the Mediterranean.

N of Carmel are natural harbors, large enough for the ships of the Phoenicians, whose chief seats were Accho (Ptolemais), and (farther N) Tyre, Sarepta, Sidon, and Byblus (Beirut); S of Carmel the shores are level to the mouths of the

P

Nile. The seaports Caesarea, Joppa, Ascalon, and Gaza have no natural harbors.

The 4 long lines above described, with their breaks and additions, render Palestine a marvelous mixture of hilly and level country, with all kinds of climate from the tropical oasis of the Jordan plain to the sub-Alpine slopes of Hermon (9150 ft.). The subtropical coastland has a mean annual temperature of 69° F. In the Ghor in May a temperature has been observed of 110° F. in the shade at noon, and 88° F. in the shade at 8 A.M. Jerusalem (3167 ft. above the sea) has an average temperature of 63° F., ranging from 39° in January to 102° in August (the greatest extremes observed since 1860); the average variation of temperature within 24 hours being no less than 51° F. These changes are characteristics of the whole of Syria.

The brokenness of the land, and especially the mixture of hill and plain, predisposed Palestine to be a land of tribes and clans. The Western Range, both S and N of Esdraelon, with Gilead on the Eastern Range, comprised Israel's proper territory. This confinement to the hills secured Israel's independence and purity. The plains and the valleys were the portions of the country open to the traffic and the war of foreign empires. Though the ancient highways of trade between the Euphrates and the Nile, and from Tyre to the Arabian Gulf, passed through the entire length of Palestine, Israel was planted aloof from all these in mountain isolation; long after her neighbors had succumbed to Assyrian war or Greek culture, Judah preserved her independence and her loyalty to the law of her God.

palm′er·worm

A name more properly applied to certain insects other than the locust (particularly butterflies and moths), but the locust is intended where the translation is used.

palm tree

The date palm. Phoenicia means "land of palm"; Bethany "house of dates."

pan′nag

Possibly a place name; other possible translations are early figs; a kind of confection.

pa·py′rus

An aquatic reed, used as a writing material in Egypt from the early 3rd millennium B.C.

par′a·ble

(Gr. "comparison") The statement of a spiritual truth, a law or principle of the kingdom of God, by means of a description or narration of facts in the world of nature or in human experience, which are represented in such a way as to illuminate facts in the world of spirit.

par′a·clete

A Greek word, applied to Jesus Christ to indicate His function in making intercession for the people with God the Father. It implies one who pleads for, counsels, strengthens, comforts.

Par′thi·a

A country on the SE of the Caspian Sea. The kingdom of Parthia, founded 248 B.C. by Ar-

P

Palm tree

The papyrus, or paper reed, from the pith of which
one of the principal writing materials of ancient
time was made

saces II, grew into an empire, and contended on equal terms with Rome.

Pass'o·ver

The feast commemorating the deliverance from Egypt. It is one of the 3 annual great festivals, and occurs in the spring; also called the Feast of Unleavened Bread. *See* Feasts.

pas'to·ral let'ters, pas'to·ral e·pis'tles

The 3 epistles of Paul in which he gives instructions to Timothy and Titus for their ministry. It is believed that 1 Tim and Tit were written after the imprisonment mentioned in Acts 28, 30, 31, and 2 Tim during a 2nd imprisonment at Rome.

Pat'mos

A very rugged island south of Samos, where John wrote the Apocalypse, having, according to tradition, been banished to it during the reign of Domitian.

pa'tri·archs

The forefathers of the Israelites. Its strictest application is to the forefathers mentioned in Genesis. A few later names are added, such as David and Daniel.

Paul

Saul of Tarsus was the son of Hebrew parents, and belonged to the tribe of Benjamin. He was above his brethren in intellect and influence, as his namesake, the king, had been in mere physique. He was born to the privilege of Roman citizenship, and is best known by his Roman name of Paul; and he used his birthright for his own protection when persecuted as a

Christian (Acts 22.25-29). He thought highly of Tarsus, his birthplace, where he was brought up as a strictly Jewish child, getting possibly some insight into pagan literature, but mainly occupied with the Hebrew Canon. At the age of 13 he was most likely transferred to Jerusalem, where his sister was, and there put under the charge of Gamaliel, the son of Simeon, and grandson of the renowned Hillel.

Saul seems to have been led into deep antagonism to Christ and His cause and stood ready to undertake a crusade against the Christian cause. Accordingly, when Stephen earned the crown of martyrdom, the young Saul did not hesitate to hold the raiment of the witnesses who secured his condemnation and stoned him; he obtained authority from the chief priests to hunt down the Christians, and prosecuted his work of extermination. As he approached Damascus on his mission of persecution, he was overwhelmed by a dazzling splendor such as outshone the Syrian sun, and heard a voice saying to him, "Saul, Saul, why persecutest thou me?" Most probably the stricken persecutor recognized the voice; but to make sure, he cried, "Who art thou, Lord?" and received an answer, "I am Jesus, whom thou persecutest." He is directed to go on to Damascus, where he will receive further light. Here his lost sight is restored, he is baptized by Ananias, and receives the gift of the Holy Ghost.

He is now driven by the Spirit, as Christ had been before him, into the wilderness, and in

Arabia he spends a considerable season in meditation. Three years enabled him to elaborate that view of Christianity now usually called Paulinism. The young rabbi at Gamaliel's feet becomes, at the feet of Christ, the great teacher of the church, translating Christianity into a universal religion.

On his 1st missionary journey he went to Antioch, where he and Barnabas were "set apart" for the work. They went then with John Mark to Salamis and Paphos on Cyprus, then to the mainland to Perga, where John Mark left them, and to Antioch in Pisidia; Iconium, Lystra, and Derbe. They reversed the route to return, and sailed from Atalia to Seleucia, the seaport of Antioch in Syria.

After a journey to Jerusalem and a conference there, Paul set off on his 2nd journey, which took him, with Silas and later with Timothy, into Syria and Cilicia, Derbe and Lystra, into Phrygia and Galatia, and into Macedonia, where new churches were established at Philippi, Thessalonica, and Beroea. There had been many stops along the way. Then he went into Athens, where he spoke in the market place, the Agora. From there he went to Corinth and Ephesus, and continued by boat to Caesarea in Palestine.

He went to Jerusalem and from there to Antioch where he lingered for some time, writing and resting. Then he set out on a 3rd journey, going again to Galatia and Phrygia, then on to Ephesus, where he stayed for more than 2 years. It was at Ephesus that there was a great riot against the new religion that Paul was preaching, instigated by those whose living was threatened, as they felt, by the threat to the great temple of Artemis, visited by worshipers from far and near. From Ephesus Paul went to Macedonia and Achaia, then to Troas to take ship for Caesarea, again with many stops along the way. He then went to Jerusalem.

In Jerusalem he was accused of taking Greeks into the inner Temple, and soldiers broke up the crowd that attacked him. His statement of Roman citizenship prevented his being scourged. He was turned over to Felix the procurator, who kept him imprisoned for 2 years. His successor, Festus, also found himself embarrassed by his prisoner, but Paul's appeal to Caesar, the right of a Roman citizen, led to his being sent to Rome. This too was an eventful voyage. Paul was allowed to visit friends along the way, and was not chained when the ship was wrecked at Malta. At Rome he was detained for 2 years under a sort of house arrest, then freed. He visited a number of the churches, but was again arrested and returned to Rome. The former tolerance was gone, and Christians were being prosecuted, having been blamed for the great fire in Rome. It is presumed that Paul was beheaded, following this 2nd trial.

Paul, the E·pis'tles (Let'ters) of

Of these we possess thirteen. They were written by amanuenses, and authenticated by the addition of a paragraph in Paul's own writing or by his signature. With the exception of the letters

P

to Timothy and Titus, which are still questioned by some critics, those ascribed to Paul are generally received as his.

These 13 letters all belong to the later half of Paul's ministry. In A.D. 52 or 53, the 2 letters to the Thessalonians were written. Then follows another blank period till 57 or 58, when, within the space of a year, the 4 great epistles to the Corinthians, Galatians, and Romans were produced. Again there occurs an interval of 5 years till 63, when the 4 "prison epistles" appeared; and finally, yet another gap, until 66-68, when he sent the pastoral letters to Timothy and Titus.

In the earliest group the second coming and the kingdom of Christ are in the foreground. The 2nd group exhibits the doctrines of grace in conflict with Judaism, and also shows us in detail the difficulties Christianity had to overcome in the social ideas and customs of the Roman world. The 3rd group is characterized by a calmer spirit, a higher reach of Christian thought, more constructive statements regarding Christ's person. In the 4th group we have chiefly instructions regarding church order, interspersed with passages of remarkable beauty and richness.

pearl

Also translated ruby, crystal. Pearls were found in the Red Sea.

pel'i·can, vul'ture

Identification of the bird intended is not definite.

Pen′ta·teuch

(Gr. "five books") The 5 books of Moses in the OT. The Jews named these, from their chief contents, Torah Law; and the Greek translators gave each book its distinctive title; hence the names in our Bible: Genesis, origin, of the world and of men; Exodus, departure of the Israelites from Egypt; Leviticus, the book of the law of the priests; Numbers, from the numbering of the people related in it; Deuteronomy, second Law. The authorship of the Pentateuch has been the subject of much controversy.

Pen′te·cost

(Gr. "fiftieth") The 50th day after the ceremony of the barley sheaf in the Passover observances. On this day occurred the gift of the Holy Spirit to the church, and for this is observed by the Christian church.

per′fume

Perfume was important in the rites of worship and as a luxury item. Moreover, perfumes were important articles of commerce, originating as they did in India, Somaliland, Persia, Ceylon, Palestine, and the Red Sea. They were manufactured and blended, and in addition to Temple incense were used in spicing wine, on clothing and furniture, and in embalming.

Per′ga·mos, Per′ga·mum

A town of Mysia in Asia Minor, in the valley of the Caicus. Near the top of its acropolis hill, 1,000 ft. above the valley, are the ruins of many temples and a great theater. It is called the most spectacular Hellenistic city in Asia Minor.

P

Per'iz·zite, Pher'ez·ite

(Heb. "dweller of the open country"?) One of the peoples found in Canaan when the Israelites arrived.

Per'sians

The Persians were originally a Median tribe which settled in Persia, on the E side of the Persian Gulf. They were Aryans, their language belonging to the eastern division of the Indo-European group. One of their chiefs, Teispes, conquered Elam in the time of the decay of the Assyrian Empire, and established himself in the district of Anshan. His descendants branched off into 2 lines, one line ruling in Anshan, while the other remained in Persia. Cyrus II, king of Anshan, finally united the divided power, conquered Media, Lydia, and Babylonia, and carried his arms into the far E. His son, Cambyses, added Egypt to the empire, which, however, fell to pieces after his death. It was reconquered and thoroughly organized by Darius, son of Hystaspes, whose dominions extended from India to the Danube. Scripture mentions Cyrus, who released the captive Jews (Ezra 1.1); Darius, who confirmed the decree of Cyrus (Ezra 6.1); and Artaxerxes (Ezra 4.7; 7.1).

Pe·shit'ta

The Syriac version of the Bible, otherwise called the Peshitta (which means either simple or vulgate), belongs to the 3rd century. The OT part was made direct from the Hebrew, with occasional reference to the Septuagint, as early as the 1st century. It was very likely made in the first instance for Jewish proselytes. There is another Syriac version made directly from the Septuagint as it stood in the Hexapia.

Pe'ter

(Gr. "rock") Surname of that Simon, son of John, and brother of Andrew, who, originally a fisherman near Capernaum, became the first apostle of Jesus. His character vacillates between obstinate resolution and momentary cowardice, as is shown in the story of his denial of his Master. In Paul's letters he appears as a "pillar" of the primitive church and the "Apostle of the Circumcision." He was married and was accompanied by his wife on his journeys. Papal claims of primacy for Peter have appealed for support to Mt 16.17-19; Lk 22.32; and Jn 21.15-17; but are set aside by such passages as Mt 20.20-28; Mk 9.35; 10.35-45; Lk 9.48; 22.26.

Peter is not mentioned in Acts after the council of Jerusalem, A.D. 50, but Gal 2.11 refers to a subsequent visit by him to Antioch. His history after that incident has been overlaid with legends. It is impossible for him to have spent 25 years in Rome, though it is probable that his last years were passed there, and that he there suffered martyrdom. It is less probable that he and Paul were put to death at the same time. If "Babylon" is not, as some suppose, a mystical name for Rome, Babylon was the scene of his labor at some period after the visit to Antioch.

P

Pe'ter, the First and Sec'ond Let'ters of

Two NT epistles. *The First Letter of Peter* was probably written by the apostle Peter between A.D. 64 and 67 to Christians who had fled Asia Minor. It admonishes the pilgrims to have hope and courage and to trust in the power of God. *The Second Letter of Peter* was probably written also by the apostle Peter but at a later time. It warns of false teachers who had come into the early church and urges Christians to be brave and patient in the midst of persecution as they look toward the second coming of Jesus Christ.

Pe'tra

The Roman name of the Nabataean city close to Mount Hor. No evidence of an Edomite settlement has been found. It seems to have been begun about the 4th century B.C.

pha'raoh

(Egyp. "the great house") One of the designations of the royal palace was "the Great House," as early as 2500 B.C. By 1500 B.C. it had become the designation or title of the ruler who lived in the palace.

Phar'i·sees

(Heb. "separated") The name given by their opponents to the party that arose among the Jewish scribes after the victory of the Maccabees, and devoted themselves to the most scrupulous fulfilment of the Law as expounded by the scribes.

Phe·ni'ce, Phe·ni'ci·a

See Phoenicia.

Pharoah Rameses II, thought to have been the pharaoh of the oppression of Israel

Phi·le′mon

The receiver of the short letter of Paul which bears his name. He lived at Colossae, where his house was the meeting place of the Christian community.

Phi·le′mon, the Let′ter of Paul to

This NT epistle is a personal letter in which the apostle beseeches Philemon to take back a runaway slave, Onesimus. The slave had come to Rome, where Paul was being held prisoner, and there had been converted by Paul.

Phil′ip

(Gr. "lover of horses") The name of 4 persons in the NT.

1. Philip the Apostle, born in Bethsaida, one of the first to be called, and mentioned in the feeding of the 5000 from 5 loaves and 2 fishes, which Jesus blessed and broke.

2. Philip the Evangelist, a Greek-speaking Christian in Jerusalem, who following the martyrdom of Stephen fled to Samaria, where he became a successful missionary.

3. Philip the Tetrarch, son of Herod the Great and Cleopatra of Jerusalem, who ruled Batanea, Trachonitis, Auranitis, Gaulanitis, and Panias with justness and benevolence. He founded and built the city of Caesarea.

4. Herod, a half-brother of Philip the Tetrarch, son of Herod the Great and Mariamne, first husband of Herodias, who in Mk 6.17 and elsewhere is also called Philip.

Other persons of this name important in the history of biblical times are Philip II, king of Macedonia, 359-336 B.C., father of Alexander the Great; Philip V, king of Macedonia 220-179 B.C.; a Phrygian appointed, probably in 169 B.C., to be governor of Jerusalem; a regent of the Seleucid state appointed by Antiochus Epiphanes at his death (164 B.C.) and quickly overthrown by Lycias.

Phi·lip′pi·ans, the Let′ter of Paul to the

Written while Paul was in prison in Rome. Philippi was an important town of Macedonia on the great highway from E to W. Philip II of Macedonia had named it after himself. In Paul's time it was a Roman "colony," a settlement of veteran soldiers. From Philippi, where he had been at first grievously maltreated, he "once and again" received pecuniary aid. The letter was written to acknowledge the receipt of such a gift. It is the most "epistolary of all the epistles;" in it the apostle pours out his heart to his friends, and entreats them to be "of one accord, one mind."

Phi·lis′tines

One of the "People of the Sea," the possessors of Philistia, the coastland from Joppa to the Wadi Ghazzeh, with its 5 cities, Gaza, Ashkelon, Ashdod, Ekron, and Gath. Though not of the Semitic race, they adopted the Semitic language of Canaan. They came from Caphtor (Crete). They were repulsed by Ramses III of Egypt after their arrival at the coast and capture of the 5 cities, until then controlled by Egypt. The Israelites warred with and defeated them, and they disappeared as a separate people.

P

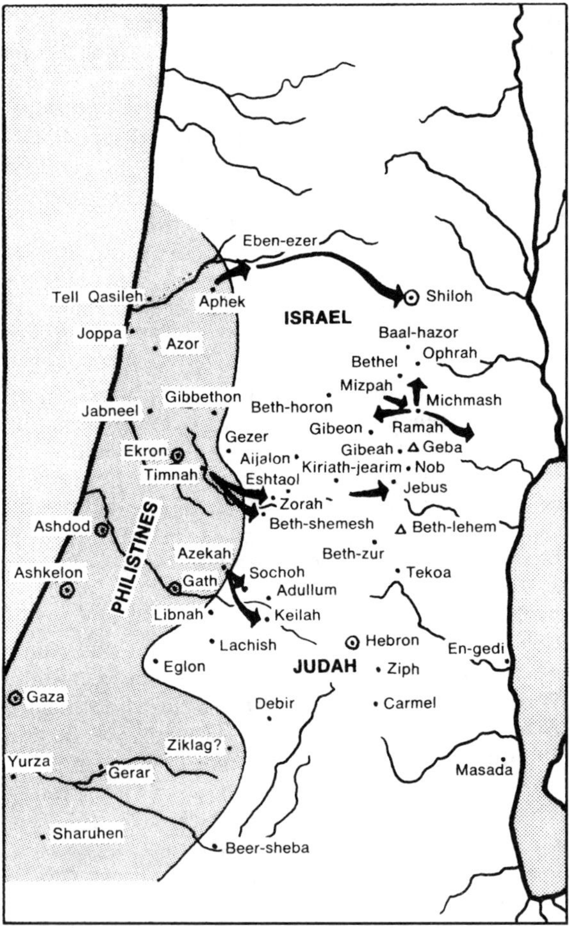
Eben-ezer
Shiloh
Tell Qasileh
Aphek
ISRAEL
Joppa
Azor
Baal-hazor
Ophrah
Bethel
Mizpah
Michmash
Gibbethon
Beth-horon
Jabneel
Gibeon
Ramah
Gezer
Gibeah
Geba
Ekron
Aijalon
Kiriath-jearim
Nob
Timnah
Eshtaol
Jebus
Zorah
Beth-shemesh
Ashdod
Beth-lehem
PHILISTINES
Azekah
Beth-zur
Ashkelon
Sochoh
Tekoa
Gath
Adullum
Libnah
Keilah
Lachish
Hebron
En-gedi
Eglon
JUDAH
Ziph
Gaza
Debir
Carmel
Ziklag?
Yurza
Gerar
Masada
Sharuhen
Beer-sheba

Phoe·ni′ci·a, Phe·ni′ci·a, Phe·ni′ce

A country stretching 120 mi. along the coast N of Palestine, averaging 20 mi. E to W. It was the great trading nation of its time, its sailors going to distant lands and often establishing colonies such as Carthage. The most valuable and profitable of many items of commerce was purple dye made from the sea snail murex. As cities were rebuilt in the same site after destruction and the sites are still occupied, excavation has been difficult. However, Egyptian objects of 3000 B.C. have been found, indicating active trade at that date. The country was prosperous at the time of Christ.

The Phoenicians are closely linked with the development of writing and the alphabet.

Phryg′i·a, Phryg′i·ans

An area and people of Asia Minor. Their boundaries shifted constantly under pressure of aggressive neighbors.

phy·lac′te·ries

Small containers, in which were placed quotations from Scripture, bound on the arm and forehead during prayer, and sometimes called amulets.

Pi′late, Pon′ti·us

Procurator of Judea from A.D. 26 to 36. Jesus was taken before him, accused of stirring up the people, but Pilate was not impressed and tried to avoid action by referring the matter to Herod Antipas. Herod also failed to act, and Jesus was returned to Pilate. Again Pilate found no fault with Him, washed his hands, and turned

P

Jesus over to the mob to be crucified, after having Him scourged.

Unverified reports exist to the effect that Pilate himself became a Christian, and Eusebius quoted earlier reports that Pilate committed suicide.

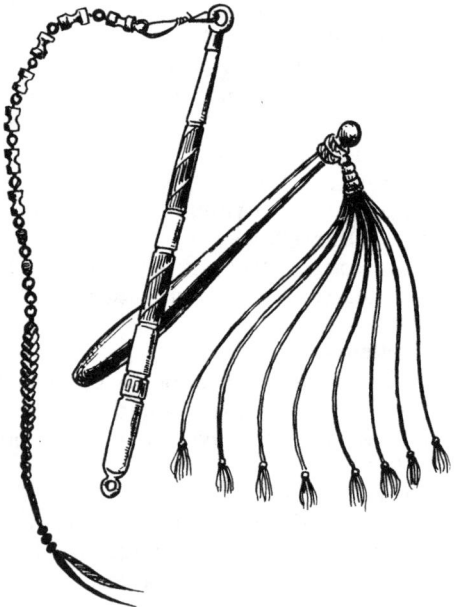

Roman scourges

pil'lar of cloud and fire

The cloud by day and the fire by night led the Israelites through the wilderness. The image may be that of cressets such as were used in Solomon's temple, which burned with flame and smoke.

pine, pine tree, cy'press, fir, wild ol'ive, box

The identification of evergreens and cone-bearing trees is uncertain. It is probable that authors of the Bible were not interested in precise botanical classification, and may not have been able to make such classifications.

Pis'gah, Mount

This is probably the present Ras es-Siyaghah, in the Abarim mountain range, and stands opposite Jericho.

Plowing with cattle, and with a camel

P

plane tree, chest'nut

As the chesnut or chestnut is very rare in the countries of the Bible, this is probably an error of translation. The plane tree does grow there.

Ple'ia·des, sev'en stars

A configuration of 7 stars in the constellation Taurus (Job 9.9; 38.31).

pome'gran·ate

A fruit found in Palestine. It is prominent in ancient art and in mythology.

Pomegranate

pound, mi'na

Greek measures, mina and lipta, and the Latin libra apparently were measures of capacity and also of weight, 12 ounces, as is the Troy pound. *See* Weights.

priests

Ministers at the altar, descendants of Aaron, to whose family the priestly office was restricted by the Levitical legislation. In later times they traced their descent from the priestly family of Zadok, the contemporary of David. The priest was subject to special laws. His duties were mainly three: to minister at the Sanctuary, to teach the people, and to communicate the divine will. His dress, of white linen, consisted of short breeches; a coat without seam, reaching to the ankles; a girdle; a cap shaped like a cup. The priests were divided by David into 24 courses, each course usually officiating for a week at a time. The "second priest" was probably the same as the "ruler of the house of God" and the "captain of the Temple." As teachers of the people the priests were superseded, first by the prophets, afterward by the scribes. The "chief priests" of the NT were the acting high priest, former high priests still living, and members of these privileged families.

The High Priest was the spiritual chief of the nation. The head of the house of Aaron held this office. He was subject to special laws. His special duties were to oversee the Sanctuary, its service, and its treasures; to perform the service of the Day of Atonement, when he was required

P

to enter the Holy of Holies; and to consult God by Urim and Thummim. It was after the Exile, and when Israel was under foreign domination, that the High Priest became also the political representative of the nation. His official garments, besides those common to the priests, were: the ephod, of blue, purple, scarlet, and fine linen, interwoven with gold thread, not otherwise identified; the breastplate, of the same material, which had, outside, twelve precious stones set in gold in four rows, each bearing the name of a tribe of Israel, and, inside, in a pocket, the Urim and Thummim; the sleeveless robe of the ephod, of dark blue, with a fringe of pomegranates and bells; the miter, a turban.

Pris·cil′la

See Aquila.

prod′i·gal son

A dramatic and vivid parable of repentance (Lk 15.11-32).

proph′ets

The books which, in the Hebrew Bible, immediately follow the Pentateuch, are Joshua, Judges, Ruth (by some considered an adjunct of Judges), Samuel, and Kings, which give a connected history of the nation from the death of Moses to the Babylonian Captivity, and all the books that we call prophetical, with the exception of Daniel.

The "former prophets" are so called simply from their position.

Among the latter prophets, the "Twelve," often termed minor prophets, have been placed together and reckoned as one book, owing to their being written on one roll.

Daniel, though a prophetical or rather apocalyptical book, is not put along with the other prophets; the most probable explanation being that it did not exist, at least in its present form, when the other prophetical books were included in the OT Canon.

Pottery from Tell-el-Obeid, near Ur, an ancient settlement in Babylonia

pros′e·lyte

(Gr. "newcomer, visitor") This word in OT times meant a person in a community not his own; perhaps a refugee, a stranger, an alien. In

NT times it had come to mean a convert. Some of these embraced Judaism completely, accepting circumcision, the rite of baptism, and sacrifice. Others were of the persuasion of the Hellenists: they were admitted to worship without circumcision or acceptance of the Jewish law.

Prov'erbs, the Book of

The Book of Proverbs is included with the OT Wisdom literature, and it has customarily been attributed to Solomon. Contained in the book are short, pithy sayings of common sense and sound advice that relate to all ways of life; in short, a practical, everyday philosophy of living.

Psalms, the Book of

The first book in the group known as the Writings. These are hymns of both Judaism and Christianity. Psalms is a collection of poems written over a long period of time by various authors. They express the heart of humanity in all generations through a variety of religious experiences. Originally the poems were chanted or sung to the accompaniment of a stringed instrument. One of the characteristics of this Hebrew poetry is parallelism; that is, the second line reiterates the idea of the first line.

psal'ter·y

This instrument is found on Assyrian reliefs. Strings are drawn over a box resonator and struck with a rod.

pub'li·cans, tax col·lec'tors

The alien government, whether of Rome or of its deputy princes, the Herods, collected its taxes and customs through speculators, who bought up the right of collecting the revenue (publicum) for their own advantage. These men were called *publicani* by the Romans. The corresponding word in the NT covers not only the tax-farmer but also his collectors. These were often natives and were classed by the Jews not only with the social outcasts but also with the heathen, as if outside Israel altogether. Christ's gracious attitude to them was therefore specially criticized and his hopeful sympathy went to their hearts.

Pul, Put
King of Assyria, Tiglath-pileser III. Also an unidentified region.

pulse, veg'e·ta·ble
Things sown.

pur'ple
This dye was obtained from a species of mollusk abundant on the Phoenician coast and produced colors in the red-purple field. Garments so dyed were of great price.

py'garg, i'bex
A white-rumped antelope.

Q

Queen of Heav'en
Jeremiah censured the Jews for burning incense to and worshiping the Queen of Heaven. Precisely what goddess was so called by Jeremiah is not clear. Ishtar, goddess of love and fertility, was so designated as was Ashtoreth, the Canaan-

ite fertility goddess. The Egyptians had a goddess Antit, called in Canaan Anat, also a fertility goddess, and all were called Queen of Heaven.

R

Ra'hab

(Heb. "wide, broad") 1. In the OT, the name of the woman who sheltered Joshua's men sent out as spies to Jericho.

2. A mythological dragon conquered by Yahweh, as mentioned in several poetic passages of the OT. The dragon Rahab was used figuratively to designate Egypt.

3. In the NT a woman in the genealogy of Jesus.

rain

Rain falls in Palestine from December to March. The beginning of the rainy season is called the "early," the end of it the "latter" rain. The summers are almost rainless.

reap'ing

Harvesting grain by hand. Barley ripened in April and May. The grain was cut halfway down the stalk by a sickle made of flints and tied in sheaves, or cut close to the head. After the 10th century B.C. the sickle blade was curved. The harvesting of all the grains required 6 or 7 weeks and the law forbade careful gleaning so there might be a share for the poor.

Re'chab, Re'chab·ites

(Heb. "rider"?) The Rechabites were a semi-nomadic people, roaming in the wilderness.

R

Red Sea

A body of water between Arabia and Africa, about 1200 mi. in length and from 130 to 250 mi. in width. The water has depths of 7200 ft. The Israelite crossing must have been at the bend of the Red Sea or through the lakes between it and the Nile Delta and the Mediterranean; there are several possible routes, but that used has not been determined.

ref'uge

See City of Refuge.

Reph'a·im

1. The dead, the Shades.

2. The pre-Israelite people in Palestine, reputed to be giants.

3. A valley near Jerusalem.

Rev·e·la'tion of Jesus Christ to John, the

This is the only prophetic book in the NT. Generally presumed to have been written by John, one of the apostles of Christ, about A.D. 95 or 96, the book is addressed to the seven Christian churches in Asia Minor, whose members were being persecuted by Roman officials. The images and illusions of Revelation are difficult for us to understand today, but to the persecuted members of the seven churches John's message was clearly one of hope, courage, and faith in times of trouble; and that on the Lord's day the faithful would be greatly rewarded. It is characterized by the use of symbolical visions as the vehicle of prophecy. The model for this mode of prophecy was set by the Book of Daniel. The theme of the Book is the gradual triumph of the kingdom of God, culminating in the Second Advent.

rie, rye

This is a grain of colder climates than Palestine. It is now believed that spelt is the grain to which this word refers.

riv'ers

In Mesopotamia the Euphrates and the Tigris and in Egypt the Nile were important to the agriculture and commercial life of the countries. Palestine had the Jordan, the Sea of Galilee, and the Dead Sea, but the people were not dependent on their river to the same degree as were the Egyptians and Mesopotamians. Palestine also had smaller streams, some of which at least ceased to flow in the dry season.

rocks

Clay, dust, earth, flint, lime, stone, and sand are words of more or less frequent occurrence in the Bible; but, as they are employed in their ordinary sense, they require no comment. It may, however, be observed that the first-named was used in making bricks, which very commonly, as in Egypt and in Assyria, were not burnt but sun-dried. In this case, straw was often added to increase the tenacity of the material. Some of the limestones of Palestine and the adjacent regions, as well as those of Egypt, afford excellent building stones, and certain varieties can be polished. The former are generally of a very pale cream-color.

rod, staff

The "rod and staff" of Ps 23.4 probably refer

to two instruments still used by Eastern shepherds, the first a heavy-headed club for driving off wild animals, the second a curved stick for guiding the sheep.

roe'buck

See fallow deer.

roll

Long strips of leather or papyrus that were written upon and then wound upon a spindle from which they could be wound off onto a second spindle as read (Ezek 2.9).

Ro'man cit'i·zen·ship

A prized possession in the time of Christ, conferring certain privileges; obtained by birth, grant, reward, or purchase. Since Paul was free born, he must have inherited his citizenship (Acts 22.27, 28).

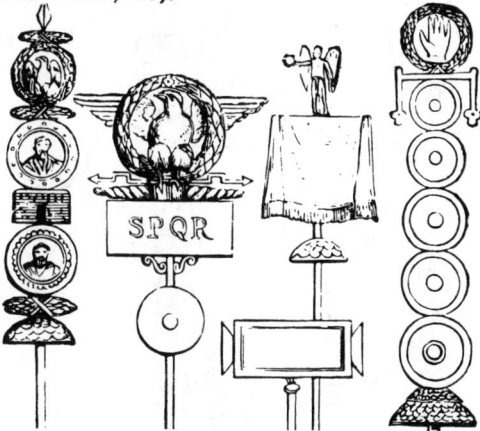

Roman standards

Ro'mans, the Let'ter of Paul to the

This book stands first among the Pauline letters, partly owing to its doctrinal importance, partly on account of its being addressed to the metropolis of the world. It was written from Corinth about 58 A.D. The purpose of the letter is to secure the active support of the church in Rome for his missionary program. Paul stresses the universality of man's sin but that God saves all men through faith in Christ. He discusses the place of Israel in God's plan of salvation and how Christians should conduct themselves.

Roman soldiers

R

Rome

A city in Italy, founded some 700 years after the entrance of Israel into the Promised Land, and at about the beginning of the ministry of Isaiah. By the time of Christ it had become the capital of an empire reaching from Britain to the Euphrates, and from the Black Sea into Africa. Christianity had reached to Rome, and there was a thriving church there previous to Paul's visit. The Jews were expelled from Rome about A.D. 50, but were soon allowed to return. It was here that Paul and Peter presumably suffered martyrdom about A.D. 64.

roof

In the East the roof is flat and usually surfaced with a 10-inch layer of tamped clay, in which grass grows in the rainy season (Ps 129.6). It is extensively used for drying, storage, and even for sleeping in the warmer months, thus needing a protecting wall about its edges (Deut 22.8).

rose

The context indicates that the true rose is not always intended; probably the word is at times used figuratively as well. The crocus may have been intended in some cases, and the oleander, the rose of Sharon. The rose of Jericho is a dried weed, which opens when put in water.

Ro·set'ta Stone

Found in 1799 in the Nile Delta, this stone had inscribed upon it the same decree in 3 languages: hieroglyphic Egyptian, Demotic, and Greek. With this key the hieroglyphic and

Demotic scripts were deciphered within 35 years.

ru'by

The true ruby has not been found in excavated sites in the Near East. The red stone may possibly be red coral, or of the nature of the garnet.

rue, dill

Rue is a heavily scented perennial shrub widely used as a condiment and in medicines. Some early manuscripts have in Lk 11.42 dill instead of rue, and dill may have been intended.

Rue

rush
Reedlike plants, found in swampy areas and along river banks.

Ruth, the Book of
The story of Ruth, a Moabitess who, after her husband's death, accompanied her mother-in-law Naomi to Bethlehem, there married Boaz, and was thereby an ancestress of David. The book is an idyll of family life, often regarded as a supplement to the book of Judges, but possibly of a later date.

rye
See rie.

S

Sab'bath
(Heb. "cessation") The Israelites apparently adopted the calendar of the Canaanites about them, related to the Babylonian Calendar described below, before the giving of the Ten Commandments established the Sabbath as an ordinance forever. After the resurrection of Christ on the 1st day of the week, that day came to replace the 7th as the Christian Sabbath. The Babylonians observed a day of rest, called Sabattu, described as "a day of rest for the heart." On that day it was forbidden to eat cooked meat, to put on fresh clothes, to offer sacrifices, to ride in a chariot, and the like. It fell on the 7th, 14th, 19th, 21st, and 28th days of the lunar month, the 19th day being the 49th

day, or 7th week, from the 1st of the preceding month. The Babylonian account of the Creation makes the Creator say to the moon: "On the 7th day halve thy disk; stand upright with its first half on the Sabbath (Sabattu)."

sab·bat'i·cal year

Every seventh year, during which, according to the law, the fields and vineyards were to be uncultivated, and their produce to be shared with the poor and the stranger and the beasts of the field. Debts of Israelites to Israelites, were to be remitted. Alexander the Great and Julius Caesar freed the Jews from taxes on the sabbatical years. After seven times seven sabbatical years there was appointed a Year of Jubilee, in which all lands that had been sold or forfeited returned to their original owners, and all slaves were set free. Though there is no record of the actual observance of the Jubilee Year, it is frequently referred to in Scripture.

sac'ri·fice

Something of value offered to a deity in return for expected favors, or as an atonement for sin or wrongdoing. Such a custom is very ancient, and is found among all early peoples. The laws of sacrifice and offerings for the Israelites are found in Leviticus. The OT rituals of sacrifice were abolished in Christ's death, the perfect sacrifice for all through all time.

Sad'du·cees

Zadokites, a party attached to the aristocratic priests who traced their lineage to the sons of Zadok, the chief ministers of the Temple from the time of Solomon. They were an exclusive caste, drawn from men of wealth and position. While the Pharisees found their strongholds in the synagogues and schools of the towns and villages, the Sadducees had their center in the Temple at Jerusalem. They were open to worldly influences of all kinds, including in later times Greek culture and Roman statecraft. Their main interest was political, and their guiding principle was to keep in with any power that secured to them their monopoly of office. They acknowledged as binding only the written Law, rejecting the traditions of the scribes; ignored the Messianic hope and the doctrine of the resurrection; and denied alike the existence of angels and spirits and the overruling or cooperating hand of God in the actions of men. After the fall of Jerusalem they lost their influence (A.D. 70).

saf'fron
Purple-flowered autumn crocus, used in cooking and medicines.

Sa·lo'me
Wife of Zebedee and mother of James and John. She saw the crucifixion and went to our Lord's grave on resurrection morning to anoint His body with sweet spices.

salt
Not uncommon in more than one part of Palestine, and abundant about the Dead Sea, beds of rock-salt occurring around its margin at various levels. Its waters also, on evaporation, deposit the mineral.

sal·u·ta′tions

Among the Jews the salutation was "Peace be with thee" and the like. The reply was, "The Lord bless thee." It was only in great haste or intense absorption that they were omitted.

Sa·ma′ri·a

A city in Palestine 42 mi. N of Jerusalem and 25 mi. E of the Mediterranean, founded by Omri about 920 B.C. as his capital. It was taken by Sargon in 722 B.C., and rebuilt by Herod the Great, who named it Sebaste. Excavation has revealed a magnificently built city, beautifully designed. The province of Samaria, the central part of Palestine, stretched from the sea to the Jordan Valley, coinciding with the land of the half-tribe of Manasseh.

Sa·mar′i·tans

The mixed population, partly of Israelitish descent, which the restored exiles found in Northern Israel. They were the hated neighbors and rivals of the Jewish theocracy. "Samaritan" was to the Jew a name of contempt and reproach (John 8.48).

Sa·mar′i·tan Pen′ta·teuch

A Qumran MS (Dead Sea Scrolls) verifies its antiquity and faithfulness of transmission, and other ancient scrolls indicate its antiquity. It is extant in MSS of very nearly as great age as the Hebrew.

Sam′son

(Heb. "sun's man") A judge or hero of the tribe of Dan, the son of Manoah, a native of Zorah, which belonged to Dan. He was a "Nazarite unto God" from his birth, the first Nazarite mentioned in Scripture. The narrative does not represent him as a leader of the people, either in war or peace; it consists of personal exploits against the Philistines.

Sam′u·el

The last of the Judges, an Ephraimite, a prophet of the 11th century B.C., who by wise administration in war and peace gained great authority in Israel, but had at last to yield to the popular wish, and resign his leadership to a king. He spent his later years at Ramah, founding and directing schools of the prophets.

Sam′u·el, the First and Sec′ond Books of

The two books of Samuel are one in the Hebrew. First and Second Samuel contain the history of Israel from Eli to the old age of David, particularly material concerning the religious and moral conditions of the period. Samuel is the great prophet-judge who helps to unite the scattered tribes under one king, Saul. The history of the reigns of Saul and David is also recorded.

san′dal

A sole of leather fastened to the foot by a strap or thong, a latchet. On the ancient monuments many types are shown, but most persons are usually depicted barefoot.

San′he·drin

The senate, or supreme Jewish court of justice for enforcing the Mosaic system of sacred law in national and civic life. It existed as early as the Grecian period. It sat under the presidency

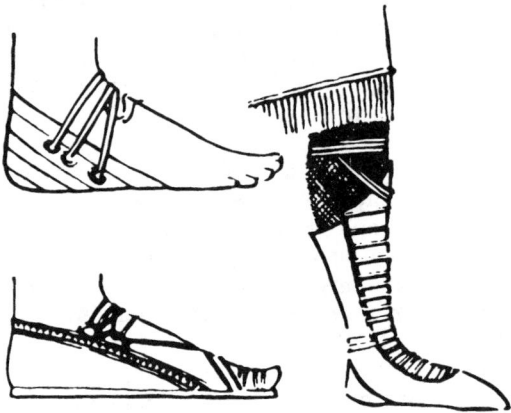

Courtesy of *The Interpreter's Dictionary of the Bible*

Assyrian sandals fastened to the foot by means of thongs (latchets)

Sandals

of the high priest, and consisted of some 71 members (chief priests, elders, scribes), among whom the priestly aristocracy generally had the upper hand, or a lower council of 23 members. It lost the power of life and death under the Romans though in moments of special excitement this limit was not always respected.

sap'phire, lap'is laz'u·li

Properly a blue variety of corundum but in ancient times the name may have denoted the beautifully mottled blue stone now called lapis lazuli. This is a silicate of various bases, softer than steel and still much valued for ornaments. It was obtained in Ethiopia and Persia. *See* Jacinth.

Sar'dis

Capital of Lydia. It was a wealthy commercial town, with a strong citadel.

sar'di·us, sar'dine

A reddish translucent variety of chalcedony darker than carnelian.

sar'do·nyx

A banded form of chalcedony.

Sar'gon

(Akkad. "the king is legitimate") Sargon I (1850 B.C.?) was a king of Assyria, listed on tablets and monuments as the 27th. Sargon II (722-705 B.C.) ended the kingdom of Israel by the conquest and destruction of Samaria, and deported more than 27,000 of its people; they disappeared or were absorbed in Media. Other conquered peoples were moved into Samaria to replace them.

Sa'ron

See Sharon.

sa'tyrs

(Heb. "hairy ones") Elsewhere the word means he-goats; but in some passages it means demons in the shape of goats, to whom the heathen sacrificed. Such satyrs are depicted on the Egyptian monuments.

Saul

Son of Kish, of the tribe of Benjamin, the first king over Israel. He fought successfully against Moab, Ammon, Edom, Zobah, the Philistines, and the Amalekites. Wilfulness in preferring sacrifice to obedience to the divine command before entering on the war against the Philistines, and violation of the curse against the Amalekites, proofs of his failure in allegiance to Jehovah, the true king of Israel, led to his rejection from the kingship. In wild fury he sought to take the life of David and massacred the Gibeonites and the priests of Nob. In the disastrous battle of Gilboa, where the brave Jonathan and two other sons of Saul were slain by the Philistines, he fell in despair upon his sword, and perished.

Stately in presence and demeanor, generous in impulse, upright in character, heroic in action, he yet showed that one act of disobedience, one instance of unfaithfulness, may be the beginning of a fall from a divine call to the highest service.

Saul of Tar'sus

See Paul.

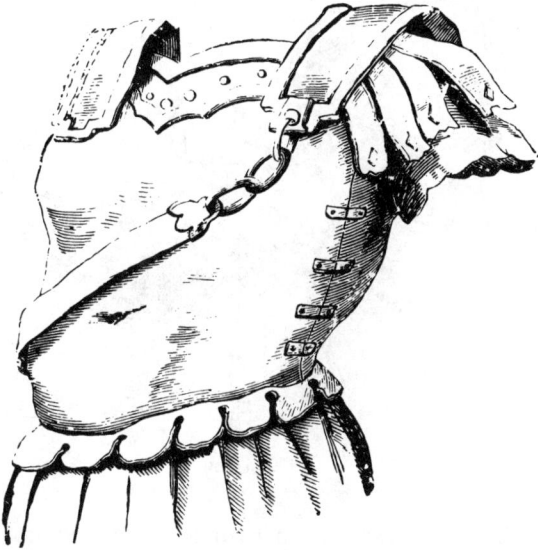

Saul's coat of mail

scape'goat
The goat laden with the sins of the people, and driven away into the wilderness on the Day of Atonement.

scar'let
A costly dye made from an insect similar to the cochineal and found in the Ararat valleys.

scor'pi·on
A lobster-shaped invertebrate with 8 legs, and a poisonous sting in the tail.

Scorpion

scribes

The "scholars" or men of letters to whom belonged the professional study of the Mosaic Law.
This special class of non-priestly Jews, beginning in the time of Ezra, had by the Macca-
baean period taken this duty under their own
peculiar care, and formed a body of traditional
law, which, though ever growing by discussion
as fresh cases arose, was regarded as equally
binding with the written Mosaic Law. Their
work included a theoretic development of the
Law to cover fresh cases; the teaching of it
gratuitously to "disciples," its practical administration in the courts, in which they sat as
judges or assessors. They were addressed as

"master," "lord," "sir" (Rabbi or Rabboni), "father."

Scrip'ture, Scrip'tures

This first was a general term, meaning simply "writing" or "writings." Then came the more precise designation "The Scripture" or "The Scriptures," as we find these terms employed in the NT to denote what were the sacred books of the Jews at the time, and we now speak of Scripture, Scriptures, or Holy Scripture when we mean the collected writings held sacred by the Christian Church.

Scyth'i·a

The country N of the Euxine and Caspian.

Scyth'i·ans

The Scythians, also called Ashkenaz, moved through the Caucasus into Asia Minor, and made raids of extreme savagery until the Medes defeated and almost destroyed them.

seal, sig'net

Like other Eastern peoples (Babylonians, Egyptians), the Hebrews carried a ring or stamp, or in later times a cylinder engraved with certain figures or characters. This being impressed on a tablet of clay or soft wax served as a signature in a country where very few could write. Sealing with such a signet was also applied to the tomb of Jesus, and to the book in Revelation. Metaphorically, it is used of circumcision, of the Holy Spirit, and of converts as the attestation of Paul's ministry.

sea mon'ster

See Whale.

Se'ir, Mount

1. The chief mountain range of Edom; modern Jabel esh-Shera.

2. A mountain 9 mi. W of Jerusalem.

Se'la

1. A fortified Edomite city, identified with Umm el Bagyarah, on the rocks above Petra, the Nabatean city. Sela was conquered by Amaziah of Judah, and renamed Joktheel.

2. Two other places named Sela are mentioned in the OT but have not been identified.

se'lah

Believed to be a direction to the conductor of the music in the Temple for clash of the cymbals.

Se·leu'ci·a

The name of 9 ancient towns, 4 of them of interest to readers of the Bible.

1. Seleucia in Syria, the port of Antioch, frequented by Paul the Apostle.

2. Seleucia in Mesopotamia, a city of more than half a million, with a considerable Jewish population.

3. Seleucia in Cilicia.

4. Seleucia in N Palestine, once important, but today unidentified.

Sem'ites

The name means the descendants of Shem, and has been given to that portion of the white race which has spoken the Semitic languages: Assyro-Babylonian, Aramaic, Hebrew, Canaanite, Arabic Syrian, Samaritan, Palmyrene, Nabatean,

Phoenician, Moabite, Sabean, Minean, and Ethiopic.

Semitic man, possibly a hebrew, from a wall painting in Egypt of about the time of Abraham. The man plucks his lyre; the donkey bears a pack, a spear, and a throwing stick

Sen·nach'e·rib

King of Assyria and Babylonia (705-681 B.C.).

Sep'tu·a·gint

The name of the oldest Greek version of the OT, made in Alexandria, which is called after the 70 interpreters who are supposed to have made it, the Septuagint (Lat. "seventy"), and commonly abbreviated by using the Roman numeral LXX. The legend of its formation is as follows. Ptolemy Philadelphus, king of Egypt, at the suggestion of his librarian, Demetrius Phalereus, sent an embassy to Eleazar, the high priest at Jerusalem, to obtain copies of the sacred books of the Jewish law, in order to translate them into Greek. Superb copies were sent, and a body of translators, 70 or 72 in number, were assigned quarters on the island of Pharos. A later tradition says that the translators were all shut up in separate cells, and that when they had finished their work, the translations were found to tally exactly.

There is no doubt that the Pentateuch was translated into Greek in Alexandria as early as the time of Ptolemy Philadelphus (284-246 B.C.). The true account of its origin is that, as there were in Alexandria many Jews who could not read the OT in the original, a Greek version was gradually produced for their use in the 3rd and 2nd centuries B.C.; probably the whole work was completed by 150 B.C. It is, as a translation, very unequal, and it has come down to us in a state of great corruption.

Ser'mon on the Mount

The address which in Mt 5–7 opens the public ministry of Jesus as the Messiah, while in Lk 6.17-49 it appears in a shorter form and at a later stage. The "mount of beatitudes," supposed to have been near the Sea of Galilee, has not been located. The Sermon on the Mount is an exposition of the nature of the kingdom of God and His righteousness. It sets forth in the beatitudes the character, and then, under the figures the "salt of the earth" and "the light of the world," the duty to the world of the citizens of the Kingdom. After showing that the better righteousness of the Kingdom comes to fulfil and carry to perfection, not to destroy, what was good in the past, it proceeds to unfold the true righteousness with regard to the 6th, 7th, and 3rd commandments. Obedience should carry beyond the language of the commandments. Ch. 6 deals with the religious exercises of almsgiving, prayer, and fasting, and shows that the Christian's relation to his worldly property is to be without greed and avarice, without pursuit of by-ends, but with a single eye, and without anxiety. Ch. 7 forbids rash judgment and profanation of that which is holy, gives encouragement to prayer, lays down the "golden rule" of love, and enforces the necessity of religious decision; then, after describing the test which will distinguish false prophets from true, and false disciples from true, concludes with the double parable of the house and its foundation.

ser'pent

In Palestine more than 30 different kinds of serpents are known, of which some are poisonous. All snakes were considered unclean.

serv'ant

See Deaconess.

sev'en stars

See Pleiades.

Sha'drach, Me'shach, A·bed'ne·go

The Babylonian names of the 3 companions of Daniel, the Hebrew names being Hananiah,

Michael, and Azariah. The 4 young men demonstrated the strength of Jewish faith at the hostile Babylonian court.

Shal·ma·ne'ser

(Akkad. "Salmanu is leader") The name of 5 kings of Assyria. The last Shalmaneser V (727-722 B.C.), besieged Samaria and died or was assassinated during the siege.

Shar'on, Sa'ron

(Heb. "plain or level country") From Carmel to some low hills S of Joppa extends the plain or level of Sharon, once covered in the N by a considerable forest, but more cultivated in its southern part.

She'ba

The name of 2 persons and a place, Beer-Sheba, mentioned in the OT, in addition to the queen of Sheba.

She'bat

The 11th month in the Hebrew calendar.

She'chem, Si'chem, Sy'chem

(Heb. "shoulder"?) An ancient Canaanite city near Mount Gerizim, 40 mi. N of Jerusalem. Abraham, Jacob, and Joshua visited Shechem, and Jereboam made it his capital. A small group of Samaritans lives in the modern town, with their synagogue on the S slope of Nablus. Excavations indicate the presence of a town as early as 4000 B.C.

sheep

The first animal mentioned in the Bible. The plains on the coast, the wilderness of the south, the rolling downs of Moab and eastern Bashan, were and are pasture lands. Sheep were used for sacrifice; otherwise slain only for feasts, or to entertain guests. Ewe's milk was the most valued product of the flock; next in value was the wool. The common breed of today, with the enormous development of fat on the tail, seems to have been the ancient breed of Israel. The Eastern shepherd's life was one of ceaseless watchfulness. At evening the flocks are folded in caves, or in enclosures on the open plain.

shek'el
See Money.

She'lah, Si·lo'ah
(Heb. "pool of the aqueduct") A reservoir of the King's garden in Jerusalem; the lower pool. *See* Siloam.

She'ma
(Heb. "hear") "Hear, O Israel, the Lord our God is one. . . ." The central confession of Jewish faith (Deut 6.4-9; 11.13-21; Num 15.37-41).

She'ol
The abode of the dead.

shep'herd
The patriarchs lived a nomadic and pastoral life and the children of Israel to a large extent continued to be shepherds after their settlement in Canaan. Mount Carmel, Sharon, the hill country S of Hebron, Gilead and Bashan were noted for their pastures. The laborious life of the shepherd is referred to by Jacob. Its characteristic features

A shepherd's scrip, sling, and pipes

are the same to this day. The dress of a Syrian shepherd consists of a shirt of unbleached cotton, with a leathern girdle, and a large cloak of sheepskin, or wool, or hair, which also serves for a blanket at night. He carries a scrip or provision-pouch of kidskin, a gourd for holding water or milk, an oak staff six feet long, and a weapon in the form of an oak club two feet long, the thick end of which is studded with nails. The shepherd stays with his sheep night and day. In the morning he counts them under his staff. Obedient to his call, they follow him to their pasture. At sunset they are led into caves or enclosures made of rough stones and the shepherd stays at night in a booth made of branches near the entrance, to be ready to protect his flock from thieves and from wild beasts.

shew'bread, Bread of the Pres'ence
The continual offering of bread in the Temple; 12 loaves, arranged in 2 rows.

shib'bo·leth
A Gilead password, mispronunciation of which by Ephraimites led to their detection.

Shi·lo'ah
An aqueduct in Jerusalem. *See* Siloam.

Shi'loh
A town of Ephraim, now Khirbet Seilum, 10 mi. NE of Bethel, the site of the Tabernacle from the time of Joshua to that of Samuel.

Shi'nar
A name for Babylonia.

Shi'shak
An Egyptian pharaoh (940-915 B.C.), the founder of the Egyptian Twenty-second Dynasty, has given, on the S wall of the temple of Karnak, a list of the places he captured in Palestine. Most of them were in Judah; a few, Megiddo and Taanach, belonged to the northern kingdom.

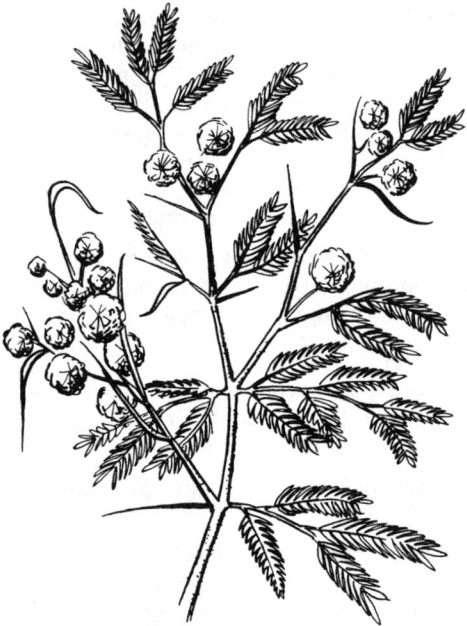

Shittah tree

shit'tah tree, shit'tim wood

A kind of acacia tree.

Shu'nem

A village in Issachar, identified with modern Solem, first mentioned earlier than 1400 B.C. It lies 9 mi. N of Jenin. Saul fought the Philistines there, and Elijah revived the dead son of a woman of Shunem.

S

Shu'shan, Su'sa
The ancient capital of Elam, in SW Iran. Its history as a city for more than 5000 years has been revealed by excavation.

Si'chem
See Shechem.

Si'don
Now Saida, a very ancient Canaanite city with a good port, center of Phoenician trade, north of Tyre. Its name is set down on monuments as early as 1500 B.C. The sarcophagus of Eshmunazar, who ruled Phoenicia and Sharon in the 3rd century B.C., was found here.

sig'net
See Seal.

Si·lo'am, Si·lo'ah
A pool in Jerusalem, also called The Pool Between the Two Walls.

sil'ver
An imported metal in Palestine, though some may have been obtained in Lebanon from an ore of lead (the sulphide), which is frequently silver-bearing. Spain appears to have been one of the chief sources of supply in ancient times. Silver was used for money and for ornamental purposes, and was well known to the Egyptians in patriarchal ages.

Sim'e·on, Sym'e·on, Si'mon
(Heb. "[the deity] has heard") 1. The second son of Jacob, ancestor of one of the 12 tribes.

2. A devout man who blessed the infant Jesus when he was presented in the Temple.

Si'mon

(Heb. "[the deity] has heard")

1. Simon Peter. *See* Peter.

2. Simon the Zealot, also one of the Twelve.

3. Simon the Pharisee in whose house Jesus was anointed.

4. Simon of Cyrene, who carried the cross.

Si'mon Mac·ca·be'us

Brother of Judas Maccabeus. *See* Maccabees.

Si'mon Ma'gus

A Samaritan magician who, impressed by early Christian miracles, offered money to Peter and John for the power of the Holy Spirit.

Si'nai, Mount

Believed to be Jebel Musa, 7500 ft., near the S end of the Sinai Peninsula.

sing'ing

Singing and chanting were a part of the Temple service. The people had such folk music as work songs, songs for weddings and other festivities and probably knew the fertility songs of the people among whom they lived.

Si'on

See Zion.

Si'van

The 3rd month in the Hebrew calendar.

slime

See Bitumen.

Smyr'na

The modern Izmir, originally a Greek colony. The old city was destroyed in the early 6th cen tury B.C., and refounded early in the 3rd century B.C. On the slope of Mount Pagus are the remains of the great theater and the stadium, close to which Polycarp, the first bishop, suffered martyrdom.

Sod'om

One of the Cities of the Plain. *See* Gomorrah.

Sol'o·mon

(Heb. "peaceful") Son of David and Bathsheba, the 3rd king of Israel. His history is narrated in 1 Kings 1–11 and 2 Chron 1–9. Under his brilliant reign the power of the kingdom reached its zenith. He stood on friendly terms with Egypt, and married a daughter of the Pharaoh. He maintained his authority over all the lands won by David and subjugated all the non-Israelite inhabitants of Palestine. His greatest achievement was the building of the Temple. He built a palace for himself, and another for his Egyptian queen; also the "House of the forest of Lebanon," an arsenal on Zion made of wood from Lebanon, and completed the fortification of Jerusalem. Not until all these works had been finished, in the 24th year of his reign, was the Temple consecrated. Solomon completed the transition of the kingdom which his father had consolidated into an Oriental despotism, establishing fortresses, increasing the army, introducing cavalry, and entering into great undertakings for the furtherance of trade with foreign nations. He formed an enormous harem, and was led away into idolatry under the influence of his heathen wives. The magnificence of his court was maintained by oppressive taxation, which, in the end, exasperated his subjects. The latter part of his reign did not fulfil the promise of its beginning, when, in the famous vision of Gibeon, he chose wisdom before long life, gold, or victory, and God gave him, besides riches and honor, "a wise and understanding heart." Along with an extraordinary power of discerning human motives, he had the gift of expressing his thoughts in pregnant sayings, which were famous even beyond his own country. There was nothing in the realm of nature of which he could not speak. He was pre-eminently skilled in that practical wisdom which, based on religion, embraced all the moral problems of life, and was the founder of the Wisdom Literature. Proverbs, Ecclesiastes, Song of Songs, the 72nd and 127th Psalms are ascribed to him. The collection of 18 poems called the Psalms of Solomon, also called the "Psalms of the Pharisees," were written in Hebrew in the 1st century B.C., and are now extant only in a Greek translation. The "Wisdom of Solomon" was also attributed to him.

Song of Sol'o·mon, the

The matchless poem of the OT is also called "Song of Songs" and "Canticles." This collection of love songs has long been an enigma and many interpretations have been offered for it. This love-relationship could signify the relation between God and His people, or that between Christ and the Church.

South Ra'moth

Ramoth of the Negev.

spelt

A coarse and inferior wheat.

spi'ces

Vegetable products used for fragrance or flavor. They were an important item of trade and of wealth, necessary for the worship in the Temple, and used in embalming.

spi'der

There are hundreds of species of spider in Palestine; that one mentioned in Prov 30.28 is more probably a lizard.

spike'nard, nard

A perennial herb with an aromatic root; a member of the Valerian family and native in India. The ointment was very expensive.

stac'te

Possibly an exudate from the storax tree or the opobalsamum; one of the aromatic ingredients of the Temple incense.

staff

See Rod.

Ste'phen

(Gr. "crown") The first Christian martyr, one of the Seven who were chosen for the special service of tables, the distribution of food to the poor. His gifts of inspired speech and miracle made him preeminent among the Seven. Accused of blasphemy against Moses and against God, he was condemned on the evidence of false witnesses. In his defense he showed by historical proof that the Jews had always resisted

God's prophets, at last had murdered the Messiah, and that the Temple was not an indispensable and indestructible institution of the religion of revelation. He was stoned to death, and "fell asleep" with a prayer on his lips which was an echo of our Savior's upon the cross. Saul of Tarsus (later Paul) was standing by, consenting to the death, and he held the raiment of those who stoned him. The death of Stephen was the signal for the beginning of a general persecution of the Christians.

Suc'coth

A city of Gad, identified as Tell Deir'alla, 2 mi. N of the Jabbok. There is evidence of very early settlement. Succoth in Egypt has been identified with Tell el-Maskhutah.

sul'phur, brim'stone

Sulphur springs and encrustations of sulphur are not uncommon near the Dead Sea.

Su'mer, Su·me'ri·an

The Sumerians came into the Mesopotamian area about 3500 B.C., absorbing, driving out, or being absorbed by the Ubaid people, who had been there from 4000 B.C. Sumer developed elaborate irrigation systems, worked out rather complicated mathematical tables and algebraic problems, had a pharmacology, a pantheon, cylinder seals, and a system of cuneiform writing. Semitic nomads, the Amorites, gradually conquered the cities and introduced their language, Akkadian. Sumer was extinct as a people and a government, and Babylonia and Assyria arose in its place.

Sun, Cit′y of the; Cit′y of De·struc′tion
Probably a city in Egypt.

Su′sa
See Shushan.

swine
Regarded by Jews (and Muslims) as the most unclean and polluting of animals.

syc′a·mine
Possibly the mulberry tree.

syc′a·more, syc′o·more
A type of fig with a leaf like a mulberry leaf.

Sy′char
A village about a mile east of Shechem, near Joseph's tomb and Jacob's well, the modern Tell Balatah.

Sy′chem
See Shechem.

syn′a·gogue
(Gr. "a meeting") A Jewish meeting-house for worship. It served for church, law-court, and school, and was governed by local elders or "rulers" who had power to inflict various penalties, including scourging and excommunication (temporary and permanent). Meetings were held in the synagogue every Sabbath, and on the 2nd and 5th days of the week. Worship was conducted by any one selected by the ruler on each occasion. The synagogues, first instituted after the Exile, were the chief means by which religious knowledge and spiritual fellowship were maintained among the people. The organization of the early Christian communities

was largely molded on the lines of the synagogue.

Syr·i·a

(Heb. "plain") The region extending from Mount Taurus to Tyre, and from the Mediterranean to the Tigris. In NT times Syria included Western Aram only. It was under a Roman proconsul.

T

tab′er·na·cle

The tabernacle and its furnishings, prepared according to the instructions of Ex 25–31 and carried by the Israelites during their wandering in the wilderness, and for a considerable period after that, was the place of the presence of God. It was a portable sanctuary, financed by voluntary gifts, that served until Solomon built the Temple. The materials to be used were available and in use for somewhat similar purposes in the lands round about; the colors to be used for the skins and hangings were also available. The tabernacle was designed to provide a suitable housing for the Ark of the Covenant and a meeting place for the rituals and worship of the people of Israel. It was surrounded by a court, also as specified, 150 x 75 ft., and enclosing in addition to the tabernacle an altar of burnt offering and a laver.

Tab′er·na·cles, Feast of

Also called the Feast of Booths, this is the celebration of the harvest. It begins on the day of the full moon of the 7th month; that is, in early October.

Ta'bor, Mount
In the NE corner of the Valley of Jezreel, 6 mi. ESE of Nazareth, Mount Tabor rises 1843 ft.

tal'ent
A weight used in Mesopotamia, Canaan, and Israel. Although it varied, it was in the neighborhood of 75 pounds. It was equivalent to 6000 drachmas (a silver coin) in NT times.

Tal'mud
(Heb. "to study, to learn") The fundamental code of the civil and canonical law of Rabbinical Judaism. It consists of the Mishna ("repetition"), i.e., the Halacha, or traditional law, as it was committed to writing by Rabbi Judah the Holy (who died A.D. 219) and his disciples, divided into 6 parts comprising 63 treatises, or 524 chapters. A supplementary work called Tosephta was completed about A.D. 400. The second part of the Talmud is the Gemara (completion), which originated in the school of Tiberias in Palestine about A.D. 250 and was completed about 400; and the Babylonian, which was developed in the school of Sura in Babylonia, and completed at 550. For the two methods of interpretation followed in the Talmud, *see* Halacha and Haggada.

Tam'muz
The 4th month in the Hebrew calendar.

Tam'muz, Tham'muz
The Sumerian god of spring vegetation.

Tares, left compared with wheat, right

tares

Weeds.

Tar'gums

When the Biblical Hebrew was no longer understood by the Aramaic-speaking peoples, just as Wycliffe's English version would be unintelligible to a modern English congregation, it became necessary for a qualified translator to give the equivalent Aramaic when the Hebrew was read. This oral interpretation or Targum was at first of the simplest kind, but it gradually became more elaborate and was reduced to writing. The Targum of Onkelos on the Pentateuch, perhaps as old as the 2nd or 3rd century A.D., became official, as did the Targum of

Jonathan Ben Uzziel on the Prophets and Historical Books, which is of later date.

Tar'shish, Thar'shish

(Heb. "yellow jasper"?) The name of Taurus, a port, far off and not identified, a distant paradise, in the OT.

tax col·lec'tors

See Publicans.

tax'es

Every Hebrew who had reached the age of 20 had to pay a half shekel for the upkeep of the sanctuary. Under Nehemiah a third of a shekel was raised from every Israelite for the building of the temple. In later times the regular temple tax was a half shekel. Civil taxes were at first unknown, but Samuel shows that they would be exacted under the monarchy. Large contributions in kind were required by Solomon; the first cutting of grass is called "the king's mowing." Money taxes were demanded only in times of extraordinary necessity. Under the Persians the Jews were required to pay not only excise and land-tax, but also a capitation tax, a direct levy on each person; and their condition under the Egyptian and Syrian rule became still harder when Antiochus demanded 1000 talents. The taxes now began to be farmed, and this system was universal under the Roman domination, during which the Jews had to pay capitation and land taxes, as well as customs.

Te'beth

The 10th month of the Hebrew calendar.

teil

Obsolete name for lime or linden tree. *See* Terebinth.

Tell el-A·mar'na Tab'lets

A collection of 296 clay tablets found at Tell el-Amarna, in Egypt, in 1887. They consist of letters to Amen-hotep IV and his father, Amen-hotep III, from various kings of Western Asia, from Phoenician and Canaanite princes, written in cuneiform characters, and almost entirely in the Babylonian language, though only 1 or 2 of their writers were Babylonians. Their date is uncertain, but may be about 1400 B.C. and earlier. Israel is identified by some with the Khabiri of these letters, who invaded Egypt some 150 years before.

tem'ple

Solomon's Temple took its plan from the Tabernacle; but its general dimensions were double those of the Tabernacle, and its furniture and decorations were on a grander scale. The Temple proper was 90 x 30 ft., and 45 ft. high. It was built of stones dressed at the quarry, and roofed with cedar. The floors were of cypress overlaid with gold and the walls were lined with cedar overlaid with gold. No stone was seen. The Holy of Holies was a cube of 30 ft. In it were 2 cherubim of olive wood, overlaid with gold, each 15 ft. high, and with wings 7½ ft long. It was separated from the Sanctuary by a curtain and by chains of gold and 2 doors of olive wood. The Holy Place, or Sanctuary, wa 60 ft. long, 30 ft. wide, and 45 ft. high. Ther were windows in its walls, probably near the roof. It contained the altar of incense, which was of cedar overlaid with gold, 10 candlesticks, and 10 tables, and was entered from the vestibule by doors of cypress. Against the 2 sides and rear of the Temple were 3 stories of rooms for officials and for storage; in front was a portico 15 ft. wide before which stood the brass

T

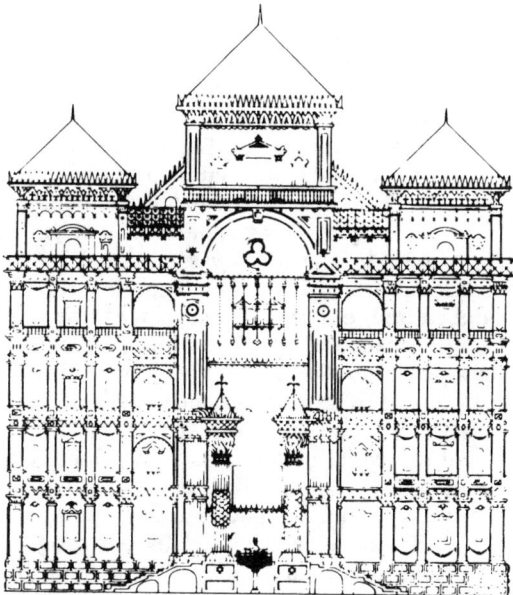

Courtesy of *The Interpreter's Dictionary of the Bible*

Solomon's temple, front view, after Schick (1896)

pillars called Boaz and Jachin, 27 ft. high with lotus-shaped capitals, or column heads. The courts of the Temple were the great court for Israel, and the inner or upper court of the priests, walled off by a parapet, and containing a brass altar, a brass sea standing on 4 groups of 3 oxen each, and 10 lavers (vessels for ablutions) of brass. The Temple was burned by Nebuzar-adan, Nebuchadnezzar's general, 587 B.C.

Zerubbabel's Temple was erected by the Jews under Zerubbabel on their return from captivity. It had the same general plan as the old, though with different proportions, and on a scale of less magnificence. Begun September 24, 520, it was finished on March 3, 515 B.C.

Herod's Temple superseded Zerubbabel's. It was begun about 19 B.C., and was not finished till A.D. 63-64. The area was enlarged to twice the former dimensions. The Temple proper reproduced the old plan, except that the height was 60 instead of 45 ft. The Holy of Holies was separated from the Holy Place by a veil and was empty. The exterior eastern end was flanked by two wings, making the front 150 ft. long. Beyond the court of the priests lay a large court, of which the part nearest the Sanctuary was reserved for men of Israel, the E portion for women. These were enclosed by a strong wall. The grand portal in the E wall was probably the Beautiful Gate. Beyond these precincts was the large court of the Gentiles, where money changers sat and traders displayed cattle for sale.

Ten Com·mand'ments
The covenant requirements of Yahweh and the Israelites, covering prohibitions in man's relations with his God and his neighbor.

ter'a·phim
Small, portable household gods.

ter'e·binth
Also called the turpentine tree; a kind of sumac, yielding Chian turpentine. It has been translated as elm, but the elm does not occur in Palestine.

Tham'muz
See Tammuz.

thar'shish
See Tarshish.

Thes·sa·lo'ni·ans, the Let'ters of Paul to the
These two epistles written by Paul at Corinth in A.D. 50 or 51 are the earliest writings of the NT. They were occasioned by his interest in the church that he had founded within 18 months before at Thessalonica, and persecution had compelled him to leave. Paul tells these Christians what sort of persons they must be, and that they must do their duty every day and not stand idle, waiting for the Second Coming.

Thes·sa·lo·ni'ca
Now Salonika, in Macedonia, at the head of the Thermaic Gulf. It was in Paul's time a free city governed by 7 politarchs. Its public assembly of Demas is mentioned in Acts 17.5. It was rebuilt by Cassander (315 B.C.), and renamed after his wife, sister of Alexander the Great, and from 146 B.C. was the seat of the Roman

governors of Macedonia. A great seaport and
the center of the Via Egnatia (the great high
road from the Adriatic to the Hellespont), it
was, after Corinth, the second commercial city
of the European Greeks, and it is now Salonika,
or Thessaloniki in Greece.

this'tle

See Bramble.

Thom'as

One of the 12 disciples of Jesus, in the Gospel
of John called Didymus ("twin"), which is the
Greek rendering of the Aramaic name. The passages in John's Gospel, 11, 14, and 20, in which
Thomas appears, reveal the intense love that
bound him to his Master. The image of the crucifixion filled his mind, and his sorrow would
not be comforted by others' testimony; he must
himself see before he could believe that his
Lord was risen. Jesus, tenderly reproving him,
granted him all that he desired; "and Thomas
answered and said unto Him 'My Lord and my
God.' "

There is an early tradition that Thomas
preached the gospel in Parthia and was buried
at Edessa. The Christians of Malabar, the
"Thomas-Christians," regarded him as the
founder of their community.

thorn

See Bramble.

thresh'ing

Lighter grain, such as spelt and cummin, was
beaten out with rods and flails; other kinds were
threshed either by the feet of cattle or by a

threshing instrument, made either of planks studded with stones or iron or of rollers spiked with iron teeth.

Thy·a·ti'ra

An important city of ancient Lydia, on the Lycus, with a large Greek population and a probable Jewish population, and noted for purple-dyeing and weaving. An inscription found there mentions its dyers' guild, among others.

thy'ine wood

The hard, fragrant wood of a North African cypress; also translated as scented wood.

Ti·be'ri·as

Built by Herod Antipas, on the W shore of the Sea of Galilee, and famous in the 2nd century A.D. for its schools of rabbis, and as the seat of the Sanhedrin, it is now a popular resort. It lies 700 ft. below sea level.

Tig·lath-pi·le'ser, Til·gath-pil·ne'ser III

King of Assyria (745-727 B.C.) and, with the name Pul, of Babylonia, 729-727 B.C. He invaded Palestine, and Hoshea, the king of Israel, paid him tribute.

tim'brel

A small drum or a tambourine.

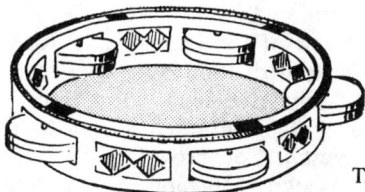

Timbrel

time

Man early recognized the year, the seasons, and the lunar month, and the calendar, made with varying degrees of accuracy, is also ancient. It was easy to halve the lunar month into 14-day periods, and halve those into weeks. Then came the jockeying of time to make the week-and-lunar-month fit the cycle of the equinox. But the division of the single day into fixed segments of time was long in coming: the hour was of variable length until the 18th century. Hence the smaller divisions indicated for Bible times are approximations only. *See also* Calendar.

OLD TESTAMENT

Morning	until about 10 a.m.
Heat of the Day	until about 2 p.m.
Cool of the Day	until about 6 p.m.
First Night Watch	until midnight.
Second Night Watch	until 3 a.m.
Third Night Watch	until 6 a.m.

NEW TESTAMENT

Third Hour of the Day	6 to 9 a.m.
Sixth Hour of the Day	9 to 12 midday.
Ninth Hour of the Day	12 to 3 p.m.
Twelfth Hour of the Day	3 to 6 p.m.
First Watch, Evening	6 to 9 p.m.
Second Watch, Midnight	9 to 12 p.m.
Third Watch, Cockcrow	12 to 3 a.m.
Fourth Watch, Morning	3 to 6 a.m.

Tim'o·thy, Ti·mo'the·us

(Gk. "one who honors God") An assistant and companion of Paul who had been trained in piety by his Jewish-Christian mother Eunice and grandmother Lois. A convert of Paul's, he traveled in Macedonia and Greece, sometimes with the Apostle, sometimes commissioned by him. He appears afterward as the Apostle's representative at Ephesus and was at Rome while Paul was in prison there.

Tim'o·thy, the Let'ters of Paul to

Two epistles, written by the apostle to his friend Timothy at Lystra, tell of the conditions in the church and describe the qualifications and duties of church officers. *Second Timothy* contains Paul's request that Timothy come to Rome to see him. *First Timothy,* which has been compared with pearls of varied size and color loosely strung on one thread, must have been written between A.D. 64 and 67; *Second Timothy* was written about 67, and is the last of Paul's extant writings.

tin

The metal (obtained only from the oxide) has not been found in Palestine. It was, however, in use, chiefly as a constituent of bronze. It was brought to the Near East by the Phoenicians and was probably procured from the Caucasus.

Tir'ha·kah

A king of Ethiopia and Egypt (689-664 B.C.) who was defeated in the Nile Delta by the Assyrians and driven S. He set up his capital in Thebes.

tish'ri

The 7th month of the Hebrew calendar.

Ti'tus

As an assistant of Paul in his apostolic work, Titus accompanied him to the council at Jerusalem as a Gentile Christian who had remained uncircumcised. He afterward appears as Paul's commissioner in Corinth.

Ti'tus, the Let'ter of Paul to

This NT epistle mentions that Titus was left by Paul in Crete to organize the work there, and sets forth the duties of the pastoral office and the virtues of domestic and social life. It can scarcely have been written earlier than Nero's persecution (A.D. 64).

To'bit

The Book of Tobit may have been written in Aramaic about 200 B.C. It is the story of the reward of a good Jew and his son for their piety and good deeds. It is placed in the Deuterocanonicals by Protestants.

tongues, speaking with

Glossolalia, which may range from unintelligible babbling to a possible higher language, opened to the Apostles in their ecstasy when, as it seemed, the Messianic age had come and they were the people of the New Covenant, with Jesus as the Anointed.

to'paz

The topaz is a fluosilicate of aluminum, generally of a resin-yellow color.

treas'ure, treas'ur·er, treas'u·ry

All wealth is treasure. The worldly wealth, the treasure of the Temple is listed in Ezra 1.9-11, 2.69-70. The royal treasures are listed in 2 Chron 32.27-29, and Solomon's in 1 Kings 10.10-29. But the teaching of Jesus was that worldly treasure was to be given up in order to have treasure in heaven. Treasuries, places where treasure might be kept, have been found in excavations, chests, grain pits in the rock, store-cities. Personal treasure might be carried on the body or buried in a secret place. The treasurer was the custodian of the treasure.

Fluted bowl and tumbler, and a spouted pitcher,
all in gold, from Ur, and about the time of Abraham

trib'ute

A payment by one ruler or nation to another as acknowledgment of submission, for protection, or in fulfillment of a treaty. Some neighboring countries paid tribute to David and Solomon, and Omri also succeeded in exacting tribute, but during much of her history Israel was in the position of paying tribute to Syria and the Mesopotamian countries to the E and Egypt to the W.

The temple tax was sometimes called tribute, because of the covenant of God and the Israelites. Census of the population with a subsequent tax was also sometimes called tribute or civil tribute.

trump'et

The trumpets found are made of gold, silver, bronze, copper, bones, or shell, with an air column somewhat less than 2 ft. In the Dead Sea Scrolls are directions for blowing a number of complicated signals. The shofar or ram's horn is not a true trumpet.

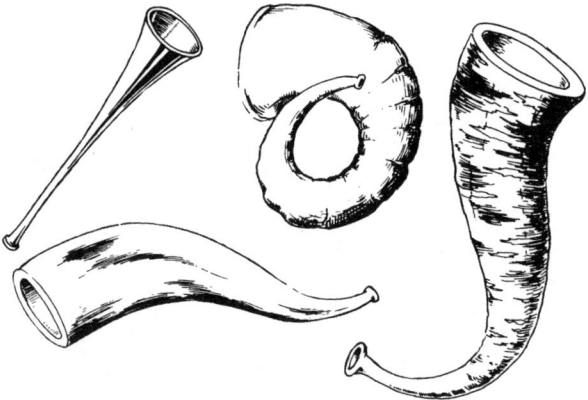

Ancient horns and trumpets

Tyre

A famous Phoenician city which, according to Herodotus, dates to the 28th century B.C. It does appear as an already famous city in the 14th century, in the Tell el-Amarna Letters. King Hiram (981-947 B.C.), who traded with Solomon and sent workmen to help in the building of the Temple, built a great breakwater that gave Tyre one of the best harbors of the E Mediterranean; it can still be seen, now under 50 ft. of water. The city was famous for its purple dye, glassware, and other manufactures, and traded throughout the Mediterranean, founding many colonies; that at Carthage dates from 850 B.C. It was often attacked by Egypt and Assyria, and was at times forced to pay tribute to one or the other. It was Alexander who destroyed it, selling 30,000 of its people as slaves, and hanging 2000 of the leaders. Tyre never regained its former prestige, and is now a city of a few thousand, called Sur.

U

u'ni·corn, wild ox

This may have been the aurochs, the extinct wild ox; the single horn of the legendary unicorn may have been derived from some account of the rhinoceros, which was mentioned in the 4th century B.C. by a writer who had never seen it. The wild ox does not appear in sculptures later than 800 B.C.

Ur of the Chal·dees'

A city in present-day Iraq, now known as al-Mugayyer, some of which has been excavated. As early as 3000-2500 B.C. it was a magnificent city, with vast temples and palaces and fine works of art.

U'rim and Thum'mim

The sacred lots placed within the pocket of the breastplate of the high priest, used in question-and-answer communication with God. The answer was usually expected as "yes" or "no." The Urim and Thummim are not mentioned after the time of David.

Uz·zi'ah

(Heb. "Yah is my might") The name of 3 persons in the OT, one of whom was king of Judah (788-742 B.C.).

V

veg'e·ta·ble

Something sown.

ver·mil'ion

Red ocher, the hematite iron ore, was used for enamel and as a paint.

vine, vine'yard

The grapevine is one of the most characteristic plants of Palestine. Noah is credited with being the father of its culture; the manner of planting, usually on a hill, is described in Is 5.1-6. A watchman was maintained, and nonbearing vines were pruned away. The harvested crop of ripe grapes were eaten at once, dried as raisins, boiled into a thick syrup, or made into wine. Gleanings in the vineyard were left for widows and orphans, and for strangers. *See* Wine.

vows

In the OT, vows are solemn promises to offer sacrifices, etc., to God in return for His help, or to abstain from some legitimate enjoyment for His sake. Such vows are voluntary and are not to be lightly made; once made, they are to be inviolate. Our Lord only once mentions vows (Mt 15.5-9; Mk 7.11-13), condemning those who give to God what should go to support their parents. Paul, at Jerusalem, took part in a Nazarite vow (Acts 21.24-26), and made or fulfilled a similar vow at Cenchreae (Acts 18.18).

Vul'gate

(Lat. *versio vulgata,* "common version") The great work of Jerome, who about A.D. 382 was commissioned by Pope Damasus to revise the Latin Bible. The result of his labors is the Latin Vulgate, of which a vast number of MSS. are extant. Probably the best text of all for determining the text of the Vulgate as Jerome left it is the Codex Amiatinus, which was written shortly before A.D. 716 either at Wearmouth or at Jarrow in Northumberland, by the command of Ceolfrid the Abbot, as a votive offering for the Pope of Rome. Ceolfrid died on the journey to Rome, and the fortunes of the book after his death are unknown; it was probably presented to the Pope in due course, and ultimately found

V

its way to the monastery of Monte Amiata, after which it is named. It is now in Florence.

The revision of the OT was made by Jerome in Palestine between 392 and 404, by direct reference to the Hebrew. The work of revision is very unequally done; some books underwent very little change, others were much more carefully treated. In particular, the Psalter, which Jerome translated afresh from the Hebrew, had already been twice revised by him on the basis of the Septuagint; these revisions are known as the Roman and Gallican Psalters. The new Hebrew translation found very slow acceptance, and the old Psalter from the Septuagint was not displaced from ecclesiastical use until the 16th century. A curious parallel to the Roman conservatism over the Psalter will be found in the Psalter of the English Prayerbook, which does not follow the text of the Authorized Version, but that of the Great Bible of 1539-1541, though frequent efforts have been made to change it.

vul'ture
See Eagle.

W

wea'sel
(Heb. "to crawl, creep, burrow") Weasels, and also polecats, are common in Palestine, and perhaps others of the genus. The weasel is included in the list of unclean beasts.

Weeks, Feast of

The Day of First Fruits, the 2nd of the 3 great festivals of the year. It is also called the Feast of Pentecost. *See* Feasts.

weights, meas′ures of ca·pac′i·ty

Weights are notable for their inexactness. Excavations have yielded some inscribed weights, and the figures offered are averages only. As throughout Western Asia, the shekel is the basic weight; there are light and heavy shekels, common and royal. A light royal shekel is heavier than a light common shekel: this in addition to the variations in weights identically marked. The averages follow.

W

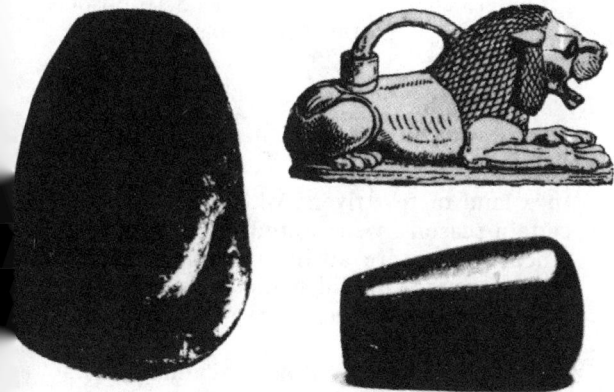

Stone weights used by ancient tradesmen in Nineveh. Often weights were made in the shape of a duck or a lion.

gerah, 1/20 shekel	8.71 grains
1/3 shekel	0.134 ounce
beka, 1/2 shekel	0.201 ounce
pim, 2/3 shekel	0.268 ounce
shekel	0.403 ounce
mina, 50 shekels	1.26 pounds
talent, 3000 shekels	75.6 pounds

Measures of capacity were never finally fixed
and discrepancies are greater than with weights.
The averages:

DRY MEASURES

kah	1.16 quarts
omer, issaron, 1/10 ephah	2.09 quarts
seah 1/3 ephah	2/3 peck
lethech, 1/2 homer	2.58 bushels
homer, cor	5.16 bushels

LIQUID MEASURES

log	0.67 pint
hin	1 gallon
bath	5½ gallons
cor, homer	55 gallons

wells

In a land of few rivers, where rain fell only at
certain seasons, wells were of the utmost importance. They were artificial ponds or pits sunk
in the ground, in which the rainwater collected
and was stored. Springs were often supplemented
with wells.

whale, sea mon'ster, drag'on, le·vi'a·than

The whale is an air-breathing, warm-blooded sea
mammal. The great fish of Jonah is not otherwise identified. Large sharks are found, as well
as dolphins and whales, in the Red Sea and the

Mediterranean. The mythological dragon and the leviathan, or sea monster, persisted in the folk lore.

wheat, corn

Wheat has been cultivated for food in the Near East since Neolithic times or longer. "Corn" as a name for a grain has in modern times been used for maize, discovered in the Western Hemisphere.

wil'der·ness

In Scripture wilderness generally denotes open, uncultivated ground, suitable for pasture, as well as desert, arid areas, and wild and rocky terrain. The wilderness of Judea, the Jeshimon, lies between the Dead Sea and the district of Hebron. The "wilderness of the wanderings" is the N part of the Sinaitic Peninsula, the W region of which is named the "wilderness of Shur" and the E the "wilderness of Paran."

wild ol'ive

See Pine.

wild ox

See Unicorn.

wil'low

Of this there are several species in Palestine. It is sometimes confused with the oleander and the poplar.

wine

Grapes were occasionally pressed by heavy stones, but usually they were trampled in vats. The quickly fermenting juice was put into jars or new skins. Water was scarce in Palestine, and the use of wine increased accordingly. It

W

was abundant in the country, and was drunk, partly as sweet must, partly after fermenting and settling on the lees. It was an old custom to add spices. Wine before being drunk was commonly filtered, to remove dregs and insects. The vice of drunkenness is frequently referred to, and there are many emphatic warnings against it in Scripture. The Rechabites and Nazarites abstained from wine. The priests were forbidden to use it when engaged in their sacred duties. A drink-offering of wine was presented with the daily sacrifice, with the offering of the first fruits, and with various other sacrifices.

win'now·ing

After the grain was threshed, it was winnowed by being tossed in the air with shovels or forks after the nightwind had begun to blow. The grain then fell to the ground and the chaff was blown away.

wis'dom

The Book of Proverbs is the earliest extensive wisdom document. Many strains of source material can be traced in it, and it expresses a wisdom accumulated from all. It contains a number of short homilies, many similies, and balanced-line proverbs. The structure is poetic and impressive.

Wis'dom of Sol'o·mon

This book, together with the Wisdom of the Son of Sirach, or Ecclesiasticus, belongs to the class of what are called the sapiential books, represented within the limits of the Canon by Job Proverbs, and Ecclesiastes.

The Wisdom of Solomon has nothing to do with Solomon, and is not older than the first (or perhaps second) century B.C. It was probably written in Greek by an Alexandrian Jew. It is a noble work, and was so highly esteemed by the Christian church that it came nearer to canonical acceptance than any other of the Deuterocanonical books. Some portions of it, which discuss the praise of wisdom, and the rewards and punishments attached respectively to the just and the unjust, have always been much admired, and some of its sentences have become proverbial: "In all ages wisdom entereth into holy souls, and maketh them friends of God and prophets"; "The souls of the righteous are in the hands of God, and there shall no torment touch them."

W

wolf
The wolf is everywhere known as the terror of the sheepfold. The wolf of Syria is the same as that of Europe, and formerly of Britain. The wolf is often spoken of in Scripture as the emblem of ferocity and bloodthirstiness.

worm
Included among the worms of the Bible are earthworms, larvae of moths, leaf-eating insects, maggots, beetles.

worm'wood
Several species of Artemesia are found in Palestine, all with a bitter taste.

writ'ing (He'brew)
From notices in the OT we learn that the Jews wrote their books with ink on rolls of smoothed

sheepskin or goatskin, with a staff attached to each end. The rolls were not written across, but from end to end, the writing being arranged in columns. When a roll was read, the beginning of it was at the reader's right hand, the end at his left. When a column had been read, it was rolled round the right-hand staff, and a new column was unrolled from the left-hand one. According to Jewish tradition, the square character now in use was introduced by Ezra. Subsequent to the Restoration, the scribes transcribed from the old character to the new such books as were written in the former. This was a task of great delicacy, because of the condition of the texts and the dangers of error. In Hebrew writing originally only the consonants of the words were written, the vowels being supplied by the reader. In such a mode of writing, the same combination of consonants may be pronounced differently. Thus, to take an English example, the consonants BRD may be read bird, bard, broad, bread, etc., and the appropriate pronunciation must in each case be determined by the context. The danger in copying such a text was that the mind of the scribe would be continually engaged on the sense while his hand and eye were engaged on the form, or else that he would slavishly copy the letters without regarding the sense; and on either hand there was the risk of mistake, all the more that several letters in both scripts closely resembled one another, and that there was no system of punctuation, nor clear spacing between words. There are many readings in the Septuagint which appear to be due to variations in the Hebrew original from which it was translated.

Y

yoke
Animals engaged in ploughing were united to one another and to the shaft of the plough by a yoke, which was a framework of wood, or wood and leather, passing round the breast of each. The yoke was always double.

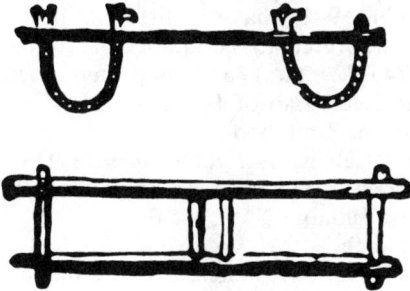

Yokes

Z

Zeal'ots
The extreme wing of the national party, in which the Pharisees represented the policy of passive resistance. From Herod the Great's time to the fall of Jerusalem in A.D. 70 they were in a constant state of ferment. Their headquarters were

in Galilee. "Cananaean" is the Hebrew equivalent of Zealot.

Zech·a·ri'ah, Zach·a·ri'ah, Zach·a·ri'as, Ze'cher, Za'cher

(Heb. "Yah has remembered") The name of 33 persons in the Bible, one of whom was the son of Berechiah, a coadjutor of Haggai in promoting the rebuilding of the Temple, who prophesied in 520 and 518 B.C.

Zech·a·ri'ah, the Book of

This OT book of prophecy consists chiefly of visions presenting motives for confidence and effort. Chs. 9–14 have a different historical setting, and refer to conquests of Tiglath-pileser III (745-727 B.C.), and may have been written by the Zechariah of Is 8.2.

Zed·e·ki'ah, Zid·ki'jah

(Heb. "Yah is my righteousness") The name of 4 persons in the OT, one of whom was the last king of Judah.

Zeph·a·ni'ah

(Heb. "Yah has sheltered") The name of 4 persons in the OT, one of whom prophesied in the time of Josiah and before the fall of Nineveh (606 B.C.).

Zeph·a·ni'ah, the Book of

In this OT book the prophet Zephaniah warned Judah and Jerusalem that the great day of the Lord's judgment is near, the neighboring nations are about to fall. He urged Jerusalem to repent, prophesied that the faithful remnant will be gathered, and the peoples will serve Jehovah with one consent. The hymn of the world's judgment, *Dies irae, dies illa* ("That day of wrath, that dreadful day"), was taken by Thomas of Celano (13th century) from Zephaniah 1.14-18.

Ze·rub'ba·bel
(Akkad. "scion of Babylon) A descendant of the kings of Judah, who was permitted by Cyrus to lead back the Jews from exile in 538 B.C. He saw the completion of the new Temple in 515 B.C.

Zi'on, Si'on
Originally the name of the fortified hill of pre-Israelite Jerusalem and poetically extended to become the religious capital of Israel.

Ziv
Second month in the Hebrew calendar.

Zo'an
A city in NE Egypt, the capital of the Hyksos and now San el-Hajar. It was once called per-Ramses, and is the area from which the Exodus began.

Zo'phar
One of Job's friends.

WHAT IS THE BIBLE?

The name "Bible" is derived from the Greek word *biblos*, meaning "book." This "Book," actually composed of sixty-six separate books, is a collection of ancient Hebrew and Christian writings, each complete in itself. The order of these sixty-six books in the Old Testament and New Testament is a logical one, giving, in general, a consecutive history of mankind—from the story of creation in the first chapter of Genesis to the visionary future of the book of Revelation.

The order of Old Testament books in the English Bible differs somewhat from the order of the books of Hebrew Scriptures. The sacred writings of the Jews were divided into three parts: (1) the Law, five books setting forth the laws which God gave through Moses; (2) the Prophets, including the four "Former Prophets," Joshua, Judges, Samuel, and Kings, and the four "Latter Prophets," Isaiah, Jeremiah, Ezekiel, and the Twelve (the Twelve consisting of twelve brief prophetical books contained in a single scroll, thus looked upon as a single book); and (3) the Writings, which are divided into four sections: (a) Psalms, Proverbs, Job; (b) Song of Solomon, Ruth, Lamentations, Ecclesiastes, Esther; (c) Daniel; and (d) Ezra, Nehemiah, Chronicles. The relative importance of the scriptural writings according to Jewish thinking is shown by this order: The Law, standing first, was considered the most important; second, the Prophets; and third, the Writings, which were truly inspired and to be treasured but were not as important as the Law and the Prophets.

In English translations of the Old Testament, the thirty-nine books may be regarded as falling into four categories: (1) History, the books from Genesis to Esther, including the Pentateuch; (2) Poetry, the books from Job to the Song of Solomon; (3) the Major Prophets, the books of Isaiah, Jeremiah, Ezekiel, and Daniel (with Lamentations, a brief and largely poetical book, regarded as an appendix to the book of Jeremiah); and (4) the Minor Prophets, the same brief prophetical books spoken of by the Jews as "The Twelve."

The word "pentateuch," derived from the Greek, means "five books," and is used to designate the first five books of the Old Testament. This section is also called "The Law" or "The Books of Moses," following the Jewish tradition that these five books were written by Moses.

The twenty-seven New Testament books are also divided into four categories: (1) History, including the four Gospels (i.e. books proclaiming the good news) and the book of Acts; (2) Paul's Epistles, the books of Romans through Philemon; (3) the General Epistles, the books of Hebrews through Jude; and (4) the Apocalypse, the book of Revelation.

Original Languages of the Bible

Nearly all the Old Testament was originally written in Hebrew; the small remaining portion was written Aramaic, sometimes called Syriac. The Aramaic section comprises three passages (Ezra 4:8—6:18; 7:12—26; Dan. 2:4—7:28), one verse of Jeremiah (10:11), and two words in Genesis (31:47, a place name meaning "heap of witness"). Aramaic was the language spoken by the people and was the language spoken by Jesus during His public ministry. However, the New Testament was written in Greek, the language used in letters and other writings. Greek was the language understood practically everywhere throughout the Roman Empire, even in the remote provinces, and was recognized as the language of culture.

Since few persons can easily read the ancient languages of the Scriptures, many versions and translations of the Bible have been made. It has been translated, either in whole or in part, into nearly every language of the world today; but, because the spoken languages change from generation to generation, the work of translation continues.

Hebrew.—All of the Old Testament manuscripts which have been found are written in square, black letters which resemble the printed Hebrew of today. These square characters came into use some years prior to the birth of Christ.

Two facts made the translator's task difficult. First, Hebrew then was written without any spaces separating the words. For this reason, the translator sometimes was puzzled to know where one word ended and the next began. Second, the Hebrew alphabet consisted of twenty-two letters, all of them consonants. (Four of these consonants, however, were sometimes used to represent vowels.) In writing, only the consonants were put down. The reader was expected to know what vowels should be added. Evidently it was believed that the reader would be sufficiently familiar with the sacred text to be able to supply from memory the omitted vowels, or else it was thought that the context in which each word occurred would suggest the proper vowel or vowels to be inserted. If we may use English to illustrate the problem, let us suppose one came upon the consonants m and n. Could one tell with certainty what word was intended? Would it be "man" or "men," "main," "mean," "mien," "moan," "moon," or even "omen."

In the sixth and seventh centuries A.D., when Hebrew as a spoken language was beginning to die out, it was observed that the rabbis were not always agreed as to the proper reading of passages in the synagogue scrolls. As a result, there was danger of confusion and misunderstanding. Accordingly, Jewish scholars of that period, who became known as the Massoretes,

undertook to determine and to indicate the
proper vowel or vowels for every word in the
Hebrew Scriptures. They indicated these
vowels by means of small marks above, within,
or below the consonants. They did not regard
these vowel points as a part of the sacred text,
and for that reason they refrained from mark-
ing them on the synagogue scrolls. They did in-
sert them, however, on other scrolls and in
their commentaries on the Scriptures.

Furthermore, in Hebrew there are no capital
letters to distinquish proper nouns from common nouns and to mark the beginning of each
new sentence. Finally, Hebrew is read from
right to left, rather than from left to right as in
English. The lines of Hebrew follow naturally
down the page, from top to bottom. In the case
of a scroll or book, one begins to read at what
we would consider the end or back, and continues his reading till he reaches what we
would consider the beginning or front.

Greek.—The Greek in which the New Testament books were written differs somewhat
from the classical Greek of a few centuries
earlier. It is the *koine,* that is to say, the everyday speech of the common people (and of the
aristocrats also) in the first century A.D. Greek
is like English in that it is read from left to right.
The vowels are included in the Greek alphabet,
and they appear in all Greek words except a
few frequently used abbreviations. The oldest

and most important New Testament manuscripts are written entirely in capital letters,
and for this reason are called uncials. As a
rule, there are no spaces separating the words.
Later Greek manuscripts are written in a running hand (cursives). Both capital letters and
small letters are employed. The latter frequently are joined together, much as in handwriting today. In the later manuscripts there
are spaces between the words and some punctuation is employed. These manuscripts come
from the ninth to fifteenth century A.D., and
they are called miniscules. The name means
"rather small"; they take that name from the
fact that they are written in small letters
rather than in capitals.

Although much writing in Old Testament
times was done on papyrus (a kind of paper),
important documents were written on carefully
prepared skins (vellum or parchment), because
of their greater durability and permanence. In
the case of a long roll, the skins were stitched
together. The New Testament manuscripts
doubtless were written originally on papyrus.
Later, when their great value had been per-
ceived, they were copied on vellum. It is not
possible to state precisely when the change
from scrolls to books took place. It did not hap-
pen all at once. It is now known that there were
papyrus books much earlier than had been supposed. For several centuries both scrolls and

books were in common use. Important books were made of vellum rather than the more fragile papyrus. A manuscript which is in the form of a book, rather than a roll, is called a codex. The word codex means "book."

The History of the Chapter Divisions

In the Hebrew manuscripts there were some indications of where the major divisions of the text began and ended. Because these sections sometimes were rather long, it was inevitable that someone eventually would make marks of one sort or another in the margins. Perhaps these marks at first merely indicated the point at which he had stopped reading. Later, they may have been added for the guidance of the reader in the synagogue, and were meant to show him appropriate points at which his reading might begin and end.

In the case of the New Testament, sections were marked off at an early date. These sections were shorter than the present day chapter divisions.

The chapter divisions usually are attributed

to Stephen Langton, Archbishop of Canterbury, in England. Langton died in 1228. Cardinal Hugo, who died in 1263, used these chapter divisions in a concordance which he prepared for use with the Latin Vulgate. Chapter divisions are found in Wyclif's versions of the New Testament (1382), and all subsequent English versions.

These chapter divisions proved so convenient when referring to passages of Scripture that Jewish scholars borrowed the idea and employed it in editions of the Hebrew Scriptures. Thus, the present-day Hebrew Old Testament has the same chapter divisions as does our English Old Testament.

THE ORIGIN OF THE VERSE DIVISIONS

The material within each chapter is further divided into verses, numbered in regular order throughout each chapter. Although these verse divisions are helpful, they should not be emphasized, for they are not properly a part of the Holy Scriptures. They should not be permitted to interrupt the connected reading of the Scriptures, especially when the passage is of a narrative or poetical character.

Most authorities hold that the verse divisions for the Old Testament were first worked out by Rabbi Nathan in 1448. A Greek New Testament, which was published in 1551 by Robert Stephanus, a printer of Paris, contains the same verse divisions and numbers which we have now in the New Testament. His Latin Vulgate, published in 1551, was the first complete Bible to contain the verse numbers with which we are familiar. The first English Bible to contain them was the Geneva Bible, published in 1560. Since then, all English Bibles have contained the verse numbers.

THE WORDS IN ITALICS

Readers of the King James Version now and again come upon words printed in italics; that is to say, with slanting letters. Some have supposed, mistakenly, that these words were printed in this fashion for emphasis. This is not the case. The explanation, really, is quite simple. The words in italics are words which do not have any equivalents in the Hebrew or Greek text. They are words which have been supplied by the translators in order to make the meaning of the sentence clearer, or in order to make the passage read more smoothly in

English. Numerous italicized words are found in the fifth chapter of Matthew, and they occur with almost equal frequency in other parts of the Scriptures.

The Geneva Bible, which was a pioneer version in many different ways, was the first to use italics in this fashion.

HOW TO STUDY THE BIBLE

The Bible is the greatest book that has ever been written. In it God Himself speaks to men. It is a book of divine instruction. It offers comfort in sorrow, guidance in perplexity, advice for our problems, rebuke for our sins, and daily inspiration for our every need.

The Bible is not simply one book. It is an entire library of books covering the whole range of literature. It includes history, poetry, drama, biography, prophecy, philosophy, science, and inspirational reading. Little wonder, then, that all or part of the Bible has been translated into more than 1,200 languages, and every year more copies of the Bible are sold than any other single book.

The Bible alone truly answers the greatest questions that men of all ages have asked: **"Where have I come from?" "Where am I going?" "Why am I here?" "How can I know the truth?"** For the Bible alone reveals the truth about God, explains the origin of man, points out the only way to salvation and eternal life, and explains the age-old problem of sin and suffering.

The great subject of all the Bible is the Lord Jesus Christ and His work of redemption for mankind. The person and work of Jesus Christ are promised, prophesied, and pictured in the types and symbols of the Old Testament. In all of His truth and beauty, the Lord Jesus Christ is revealed in the gospels; and the full meanings of His life, His death, and His resurrection are explained in the epistles. His glorious coming again to this earth in the future is unmistakably foretold in the book of Revelation. The great purpose of the written Word of God, the Bible, is to reveal the living Word of God, the Lord Jesus Christ (read John 1:1-18).

Dr. Wilbur M. Smith relates seven great things that the study of the Bible will do for us:

1. **The Bible discovers and convicts us of sin.**
2. **The Bible helps cleanse us from the pollutions of sin.**
3. **The Bible imparts strength.**
4. **The Bible instructs us in what we are to do.**
5. **The Bible provides us with a sword for victory over sin.**
6. **The Bible makes our lives fruitful.**
7. **The Bible gives us power to pray.**

You do not need a whole library of books to study the Bible. The Bible itself is its own best commentator and explanation.

I. PERSONAL BIBLE STUDY
A. Devotional Bible Study

The Bible is not an end in itself but it is a means to the end of knowing God and doing His will. God has given us the Bible in order that we might know Him and that we might do His will here on earth.

Therefore devotional Bible study is the most important kind of Bible study. Devotional Bible study means reading and studying the Word of God in order that we may hear God's voice personally and that we may know how to do His will and to live a better Christian life.

For your devotional reading and study of the Bible, here are several important, practical suggestions:

1. Begin your Bible reading with prayer. **(Ps. 119:18; John 16:13, 14, 15)**.

2. Take brief notes on what you read. Keep a small notebook for your Bible study (see no. 4).

3. Read slowly through one chapter, or perhaps two or three chapters, or perhaps just one paragraph at a time. After reading, ask yourself what this passage is about. Then reread it.

4. It is often very helpful in finding out the true meaning of a chapter or passage to ask yourself the following questions, and then write the answers simply in your notebook:

    a. What is the main subject of this passage?

    b. Who are the persons revealed in this passage: Who is speaking? About whom is he speaking? Who is acting?

    c. What is the key verse of this passage?

    d. What does this passage teach me about the Lord Jesus Christ?

    e. Is there any sin for me to confess and forsake in this passage?

    f. Is there any command for me to obey in this passage?

    g. Is there any promise for me to claim?

    h. Is there any instruction for me to follow?

    i. Is there any prayer that I should pray?

Not all of these questions may be answered in every passage.

    5. Keep a spiritual diary. Either in your Bible study notebook mentioned above (no. 2), or in a separate notebook entitled, "My Spiritual Diary," write down daily what God says to you through the Bible. Write down the sins that you confess or the commands you should obey that are mentioned above.

    6. Memorize passages of the Word of God. Write verses on cards with the reference on one side and the verse on the other. Carry these cards in your pocket and review them while you're waiting for a train, standing in lunch line, etc.

    Other person prefer to memorize whole passages or chapters of the Bible. A small pocket Bible will help you to review these passages when you have spare moments. One of the best ways is to spend a few minutes every night before going to sleep, in order that your subconscious mind may help you fix these passages of God's Word in your mind while you're asleep. **(Ps. 119:11).**

To meditate means "to reflect, to ponder, to consider, to dwell in thought," Through meditation the Word of God will become meaningful and real to you, and the Holy Spirit will use this time to apply the Word of God to your own life and its problems.

7. Obey the Word of God. As Paul said to Timothy in 2 Tim. 3:16, "All scripture is given by inspiration of God, and is profitable for doctrine, for reproof, for correction, for instruction in righteousness." The Bible has been given to us that we may live a holy life, well-pleasing unto God.

8. The Navigators, a group of men banded together just before World War II to encourage. Bible study among Christian servicemen, has developed a splendid plan for a personal, devotional study.

   a. After prayer, read the Bible passage through slowly once silently, and then read it again aloud.

   b. In a large notebook divide the paper into columns and head each column as follows: Chapter title, Key verse, Significant truth, Cross-references, Difficulties in this passage (personal or possible), Application to me, and Summary or outline of the passage. In each of these columns write the information desired.

Do not try to adopt all of these methods at once, but start out slowly, selecting those methods and suggestions which appeal to you. You will find, as millions of others have done before you, that the more you read and study the Word of God, the more you'll want to read it. Therefore the following suggestions of Bible study are made for those who wish to make a more intensive study of the Bible truths.

B. Study for Bible Knowledge

There are many valuable methods of Bible study. One may study the Bible to see the great truths which stand out in every book. Or one may study the Bible to find all of the marvelous details which are in this mine of spiritual riches. In this section there are several proven methods by which a person may do more intensive Bible study. The most important thing is to follow faithfully some systematic method of Bible study.

1. *Bible Study by Chapters.*

In the Bible there are 1,189 chapters in the Old and New Testaments. In a little over three years a person could make an intensive study of the whole Bible, just taking a chapter a day. It is usually a good practice to start your Bible study in the New Testament.

a. Read through the chapter carefully, seeking to find its main subject or subjects.

b. As you read each chapter, give it a title which suggests its main content.

c. Reread the chapter again and make a simple outline of it which will include its main thoughts.

d. Concerning each chapter, ask and answer the questions suggested in item number 4 of devotional Bible study hints above. Especially take note of any practical or theological problems in this chapter. Then using your concordance look up the key words in those verses and find out what other portions of the Bible will have to say about this question or problem. Compare Scripture with Scripture to find its true meaning. Very often to understand an important Bible chapter, one must study it together with the preceding or following chapters.

2. *Bible Study by Paragraphs.* A paragraph is a unit of thought in writing, usually containing several sentences. When an author changes his subject of emphasis in his writing, he usually begins a new paragraph. Studying the Bible by paragraphs like this is often called analytic Bible study.

a. Read the paragraph carefully for its main thought or subject.

b. In order to find the relation of the important words and sentences in this paragraph, it is often helpful to rewrite the text in paragraph form.

c. From the text which you've now rewritten so that you can see the relationship of the various parts of the paragraph, it is easy to make a simple outline

d. It is helpful also to look up important words in the concordance that occur in this paragraph.

3. *Bible Study by Verses.* In studying the historical passages of the Bible, such as much of the Old Testament or parts of the gospels, each verse may have only one simple meaning.

But many verses in both the Old and New Testaments are rich with many great Bible truths which will demand more detailed study. There are many ways that you can study a single Bible verse.

a. Study it by the verbs in the verse. For example, if you were studying **John 3:16,** you would find the following verbs: "loved, gave . . . should not perish . . . hath . . ."

Or simply take the nouns in this wonderful verse: "God . . . world . . . only begotten Son . . . whosoever . . . everlasting life."

b. Study a verse through the personalities revealed. For example, once again taking John 3:16, these very simple but significant points are brought to light: "God . . . only begotten Son . . . whosoever . . . Him."

c. Study a verse by looking for the great ideas revealed in it.

d. Sometimes a combination of these various ideas applied to a verse will bring the richest results.

4. *Bible Study by Books.* After you have begun to study the Bible by chapters or paragraphs or verses, you will be ready to study the Bible by books.

a. There are several methods of Bible book study.

(1) One is called the inductive method of studying in detail the contents of a Bible book and then drawing from these details general conclusions or principles concerning the contents and purpose of the book.

(2) Another method of book study is called the synthetic method. By this

method, one reads the Bible book over several times to receive the general impressions of the main ideas and purpose of the book without attention to the details. (It is sometimes hard to distinguish these two methods.)

(3) In some case the study of a Bible book becomes a historical study, if that book relates the history of a nation or a man in a particular period of time. For example, the book of Exodus tells the history of the children of Israel from the death of Joseph in Egypt until the erection of the tabernacle in the wilderness under Moses. This covers approximately 400 years.

The principles for Bible book study, whether inductive or synthetic, are very similar. Such study will require more time than the previous methods mentioned, but it will be amply rewarding to you.

b. Here are some methods for Bible study by books:

(1) Read the book through to get the mood, the sweep, and the general emphasis of the book.

(2) Reread the book many times, each time asking yourself one main question and jotting down the answers you find as you read. Here are the most important questions to ask:

First Reading
What is the central theme or emphasis of this book? What is the key verse in this book?

Second Reading
Remembering the theme of the book, see how it is emphasized and developed in the book. Look for any special problems or applications to this theme.

Third Reading
What does this book tell me about the author and his circumstances when he wrote?

Fourth Reading
What does the book tell me about the people to whom the book was written and their circumstances, need, or problems?

Fifth Reading
What are the main divisions of the book? Is there any outline apparent in the logical organization and development of the book? During this reading, it is now time to divide the text into the paragraphs as you see them and then give a title to each paragraph.

Sixth and Successive Readings
Look for other facts and/or information that your earlier reading has suggested. By now certain words will stand out in the book. See how often they recur.

As you read and reread a book, you'll

find soon that you begin to see its structure and its outline very clearly. It is true, however, that there are many more than one possible outline for any given book. It depends on the principle of division that you select.

5. *Bible Study by Words.* There are two profitable and helpful ways of studying great words or subjects in the Word of God.

   a. Word study by Bible books. Certain words have special significance in certain Bible books. For example, after studying the Gospel of John as a book and by chapters, you'll find it instructive and inspiring to trace the word "believe" or "belief." It occurs almost 100 times.

   b. General word study. The fine index and concordance which you'll find in this Bible will be a great help. By the study of great Bible words anyone can soon become familiar with the great doctrines of the Bible and understand the great theological principles which the Bible reveals.

6. *Bible Study by Topics.* Closely related to the method of study by words, is the study according to great topics or subjects: Bible prayers, Bible promises, Bible sermons, Bible songs, Bible poems, etc.

Or one might study Bible geography by reading rapidly through and looking for rivers, seas, mountains, etc., highlighted in Scripture. For example, the mountain top experiences in the life of Abraham are a thrilling study.

Another challenging study is to read rapidly through the Gospels and epistles looking for the commands of the Lord to us. The list of Bible topics is unlimited.

First, for a topical study on prayer, look up the word "prayer," "pray," etc., in your concordance. Look up every form of these words and such related words as "ask," "intercession," etc. After you have looked up these verses, study them and bring together all the teaching on prayer that you find. You will find: conditions of prayer, words to be used in prayer, results to expect from prayer, when to pray, where to pray, etc.

7. *Bible Study Through Biography.* The Bible is a record of God's revealing Himself to men and through men. The Old Testament as well as the New is rich in such biographical studies.

Let us summarize various methods for studying the great Bible biographies:
   a. Read the Bible book or passages in which this person's life is prominent,

e.g., Abraham in **Gen. 12-25**, plus references to Abraham in **Heb. 11** and **Rom. 4**.

b. Trace character with your concordance.

c. Be careful to note indirect references to the man or his life in other portions of Scripture.

8. *Conclusion.* There are many other methods of studying the Bible: the psychological method, the sociological method, the cultural method, the philosophical method, etc. However, the methods given above largely include all these other methods.

Use all the Bible study methods suggested above. From time to time change your method so that you'll not become too accustomed to any one method, or tired from delving too deeply into one type of study.

The great thrill of Bible study is discovering these eternal truths of God's Word for yourself and embarking on the adventure of obeying them and experiencing the blessing in your personal life.

II. FAMILY BIBLE STUDY

Nothing is more important in a Christian home than the family altar. At a convenient time when all members of the family are home, father or mother should lead them in worship of God and in reading His Word. A simple program for family worship includes singing a hymn, an opening prayer by a family member, a brief Bible study and a concluding period of prayer in which all members take part.

The family altar and Bible study will bind the family togetrher, eliminate juvenile delinquency, foster deeper love, and enable each member to become a stronger, better Christian.

Since family Bible study usually includes small children, it is wise to avoid deep, difficult topics and study something of interest and help to all. Such subjects might be Bible biographies as outlined above, stories of miracles and deeds of Jesus as revealed in the Gospels, miracles in the Old Testament, and other narrative portions of the Bible. It is wise to keep the study brief and concentrate on a short passage of Scripture. For example, if the family is going to study the life of Moses, it could be divided into units like this:

First day: The birth of Moses: Exodus 2:1-10
Second day: Moses' great choice and great mistake: Heb. 11:24-27; Ex. 2:11-15
Third day: Moses' wilderness training:
    Ex. 2:16-25
Fourth day: Moses' call to serve God:
    Ex. 3:1-22

Fifth day: Moses' argument with God:
   Ex. 4:1-17
Sixth day: Moses' return to Egypt:
   Ex. 4:18-31, etc.

Here are several practical hints on how to make your family Bible study interesting and profitable to all:

1. Keep your family Bible study reasonably short: one brief chapter or several paragraphs a day.

2. Have each member read a verse.

3. Appoint one family member to lead in worship each day and select the passage to read. This one may appoint others to help in the family worship.

4. Read through a Bible book, a chapter or several paragraphs each day. As you read, together decide on a name or a title for each chapter and memorize this.

5. After reading the passage, have each member in the family explain one verse or one paragraph.

6. Let the leader (or the father or mother) prepare five or ten questions on the Bible passage and ask various members of the family to answer these questions after the passage has been read.

7. Study the maps in your Bible together and trace Paul's journeys, or the wandering of the children of Israel in Egypt.

8. Study Bible topics together. Assign

verses concerning a topic or great word to each member of the family. Let each read this verse and tell what his verse teaches about his topic or word.

9. After the Bible reading, have each member tell what this verse means to him or how he believes it can be applied to his life.

10. Make up Bible games by having each member make up questions to try to stump the others.

11. Study a Bible book together, using the hints given above. There are many wonderful ways to make the Bible the heart of your home.

III. PRINCIPLES OF BIBLE INTERPRETATION

Since the Bible was written by many men over a period covering 1,500 years; and since the last author of the Bible has been dead 1,900 years, there are definite problems in understanding the exact meaning of certain passages of the Bible.

There is a need to interpret clearly certain passages of the Bible because there is a gap between the way we think and the words we use today and the way of thinking and the words that these Bible writers used thousands of years ago. Bible scholars have pointed out that there are language gaps—differences in words that we use; there are cultural gaps—different

customs were in vogue then. There are geographical gaps—certain rivers that are spoken
of in the Bible have long since dried up. Some
places that are spoken of frequently in the
Bible are not on our modern maps. And then
there are historical gaps—the Bible speaks of
kings and empires which existed years ago.

Therefore there is a need for Bible interpretation. This is a fascinating study in itself, but I
want to give you just a few principles of interpretation of the Bible that will keep you from
error and help you to understand the difficult
passages of the Word of God.

1. Always remember that the Bible is God's
   infallible, inerrantly inspired word. There
   are no mistakes in the Bible. God has included everything in the Bible that He
   wants you to know and that is necessary
   for you to know concerning salvation and
   your Christian life.
2. The second principle of interpretation is
   to interpret the Bible in the light of its historical background. There are three as-
   pects of this:
   a. Study the personal circumstances of
      the writer.
   b. Study the culture and customs of the
      country at the time that the writing or
      story was taking place.
   c. Study and interpret the Bible in the
      light of the actual historical situation

and events that were taking place at
the time of the story.

3. Interpret the Bible according to the purpose and plan of each book.

Every Bible book has its specific purpose intended by the Holy Spirit to bring
some special message to man.

4. One of the most important principles of
interpretation is always to interpret according to the context of a verse.

The "context" is the verses immediately preceding and immediately following the verse you are studying. If you do
not take care to interpret the verse according to the context, you could make the
Bible teach atheism. For the Bible itself
says, "there is no God" **(Psalms 14:1)**. But
the context makes very clear what this
verse means: The immediately preceding
sentence says, "the *fool* hath said in his
heart, 'there is not God.' "

Always study the passage immediately
preceding and immediately following any
verse, word, or topic to make sure that
you see this truth in the setting which God
intended.

5. Interpret always according to the correct
meaning of words. You can find the correct meaning of a word in several ways.
First of all look up the usage of the word
in other parts of the Bible to find how it

was used in that generation. Another way is to look up its background or its root. You could do this with the use of a dictionary. Still another way is to look up the synonyms—words that are similar in meaning but slightly different: for example, "prayer," "intercession," "supplication."

6. Interpret the Bible also according to all of the parallel passages which deal with the subject, and according to the message of the entire Bible.

The more you read the Bible, the more you will understand that in it God is revealing His way of salvation to men from beginning to end. And when you come to a difficult passage, think of it in the light of the overall purpose of the Bible. For example, the animal sacrifices of the Old Testament are meant to be a picture of the perfect sacrifice of Jesus Christ on the cross.

If you will follow these simple rules, you will be kept from error and extremes, and you will be helped to understand correctly the teachings of even the more difficult passages in God's Word.